Food and
Transformation

Marie-Louise von Franz, Honorary Patron

**Studies in Jungian Psychology
by Jungian Analysts**

Daryl Sharp, General Editor

Food and Transformation

Imagery and Symbolism
of Eating

Eve Jackson

Canadian Cataloguing in Publication Data

Jackson, Eve, 1943-
  Food and transformation: imagery and symbolism of eating

(Studies in Jungian psychology by Jungian analysts; 74)

Includes bibliographical references and index.

ISBN 0-919123-75-9

1. Food—Psychological aspects.
2. Food habits—Psychological aspects.
I. Title. II. Series.

TX357.J33 1996   641.3'0019   C96-930171-5

INNER CITY BOOKS
Box 1271, Station Q, Toronto, Canada M4T 2P4
Telephone (416) 927-0355
FAX 416-924-1814

Honorary Patron: Marie-Louise von Franz.
Publisher and General Editor: Daryl Sharp.
Senior Editor: Victoria Cowan.

INNER CITY BOOKS was founded in 1980 to promote the
understanding and practical application of the work of C.G. Jung.

Cover painting and illustrations on pages 10, 91, 117
by Vicki Cowan (Copyright © 1996).

Index by Daryl Sharp

Printed and bound in Canada by
University of Toronto Press Incorporated

CONTENTS

See final page for descriptions of other Inner City Books

Acknowledgments

I would like to thank warmly all those analysands, colleagues and friends who kept the developing book fed with stories, dreams and suggestions. I am especially indebted to Dave Stevens, who provided me with hot dinners while I wrote, and to Molly Tuby, for her many helpful comments on the manuscript.

The story "The Lion's Share" on page 59, from *The King's Drum and Other African Stories* by Harold Courlander (published by Rupert-Hart Davis, an imprint of HarperCollins Publishers Limited), is used with permission.

Food, eat, eating . . . *verbs*—eat, feed, fare, devour, swallow, take; gulp, bolt, snap; fall to; despatch, dispatch; take down, get down, gulp down; lay in, tuck in; lick, pick, peck; gormandize (see gluttony); bite, champ, munch, crunch, chew, masticate, nibble, gnaw; live on; feed on, batten on, fatten on, feast upon; browse, graze, crop; regale, carouse; eat heartily, do justice to; banquet; break bread, break one's fast; breakfast, lunch, dine, take tea, sup. *Colloq.,* put away; drink like a fish; come and get it! soup's on!
　　　　　　　　　　—Roget's *Thesaurus.*

Introduction

What we call the outer world meets us via the senses with its colors, textures, smells, distances, its high and low, fast and slow, its growing, dying, running, flying, fighting, eating and so on, ad infinitum. Our inner life also has its intensities of experience, its darting thoughts and shifting feelings. Beyond those immediately recognizable experiences there is a vast realm of unconscious psychic activity which we glimpse in dreams and fantasy. The imagination clothes those otherwise imperceptible movements in forms borrowed from outer life, those colors, textures, highs and lows and so forth, often recombined in curious ways.

> It is not the world as we know it that speaks out of [the] unconscious, but the unknown world of the psyche, of which we know that it mirrors our empirical world only in part, and that, for the other part, it moulds this empirical world in accordance with its own psychic assumptions.[1]

The natural language of the psyche is metaphorical, making use of the image as carrier of new meaning. A dream may point to known persons and situations, but much of the time it is playing a teasing game of "as if" as the best way of communicating the psychic unknown to consciousness; if we take it literally the point is lost. At the collective level, myths and fairy stories, in their more organized fashion, seemingly speak of outer events that happened once upon a time, but they also confront us with figures never found in empirical nature—giants, nymphs, talking animals and magic rings that exist at another level of reality. In the apparent chaos of alchemical texts Jung discovered a wealth of the same kind of imagery that shapes certain dreams.

Just where the boundary lies between inner and outer, between

---

[1] "The Psychology of the Child Archetype," *The Archetypes and the Collective Unconscious,* CW 9i, par. 260. [CW refers to *The Collected Works of C.G. Jung]*

literal and symbolic, is no easy matter to ascertain, for our experiences in the sense world trigger associative and symbolizing processes in the psyche, and the metaphorical images that arise within project themselves so convincingly onto outer circumstances that we are constantly deceived. Ultimately inner and outer, physical and psychic, are aspects of one encompassing reality, yet consciousness requires of us that we distinguish between them.

In writing about the vast subject of food and eating I have tried to keep constantly in mind the interplay of conscious and unconscious, physical and psychic, literal and metaphorical, but above all I have tried to listen to what the *psyche* has to say through the medium of dreams, myths and customs, and through the half-hidden images incorporated in language.

In contemporary Western society there is a great deal of unease about food. This is all too natural when provisions are scarce and uncertain, as has been the case throughout most of our history, and remains so in many parts of the world as well as in the poorest sections of our society. It is hard not to have food on your mind when you are constantly hungry or threatened with hunger. To the hungry person a plentiful food supply implies a great liberation, an opportunity to focus on concerns other than the next meal. In what has been dubbed the consumer society, however, maniacally gobbling the earth's resources and presenting us with ever-expanding sets of choices, new food-related anxieties have arisen. Respite from externally imposed famine means that we are all the freer to project meanings onto food that have nothing to do with assuaging our alimentary needs, seeking through eating to satisfy our longing for affection or sexual fulfillment, or to muffle our grief or rage. Food can also become the repository of our secret fears and our fantasies of perfect health.[2]

The great triumph of controlling nature to the extent of obliging her to produce a steady abundance of food has not been a once-and-for-all achievement. She has infinite ways of slipping out of our at-

---

[2] On this subject see Hilde Bruch, *Eating Disorders,* chap. 4.

tempts to control her and presenting us with new challenges. For many people fear of famine has been replaced by fear of poisoning from inorganic fertilizers, pesticides, additives, irradiation and genetic manipulation. While these fears have valid grounds, they can merge all too easily with our neuroses through the projection of the hidden poisons and dark conflicts of the unconscious psyche. Thus we demonize food or alternatively seek out the one magical ingredient (fiber, polyunsaturated fat, wheat germ, royal jelly) that will make us whole. Jung observed in 1930:

> People who get wrong psychologically are often health fanatics. They are always seeking the right food and the right drinks, they don't smoke and they don't drink wine, they need a lot of salts and are drug-store fiends. Always some new scheme and never very healthy.[3]

Equally striking is the fear of fatness and the prevalence of eating disorders which are unimaginable in societies where procuring an adequate food supply is a central issue. But this is not a book on eating disorders or dietary problems. That is a highly complex area in itself, with numerous ramifications, a few of which are just touched on in the short final chapter.

My exploration of the subject of food and eating was stimulated by interest in the complex meanings we attach to food, and in the paradoxical sufferings of plenty, particularly as encountered through the practice of psychotherapy. When the psyche talks about food, about feeding, nourishing, starving, taste, assimilation, it is generally not to be taken literally. References to particular foodstuffs need to be evaluated in terms of individual and collective associations. The latter are deeply ingrained in culture and may hark back to the experiences of our Paleolithic ancestors and beyond. In exploring the psychic background of food we also begin to understand how the literal process of eating is affected by symbolic associations and metaphoric attributions, and by the constant interplay between conscious and unconscious.

---

[3] *Dream Analysis,* p. 459.

1
The Food Chain

We are what we eat.—Ludwig Feuerbach.

In the cyclic process of transformation on the earth's surface, plants assimilate nutrients from the mineral world, animals devour vegetables and each other, and animal and vegetable remains fall back into inert matter, swallowed by the earth, sometimes first consumed by fire. The biological species, each separately reproducing, are all intimately interconnected through the endless alimentary chain. "From first to last, the question has not been 'To be or not to be?' but 'To eat or to be eaten?' of which desire and terror are the effects."[4] On this wheel we are all bound.

Through this constant transformation of substance the earth maintains her stability and the continuity of life. In his scientific evocation of the great goddess Gaia—according to Hesiod the mother of all beings[5]—James Lovelock writes:

> It can now be demonstrated, with the aid of numerical models and computers, that a diverse chain of predators and prey is a more stable and stronger ecosystem than a single, self-contained species, or a small group of very limited mix.[6]

Lovelock sees this relationship as a function of the earth's self-regulating and therefore living system. Mother Nature provides caterpillars for birds and leaves for caterpillars, fish for otters and little fish for big fish, and through them she lives her own life, regulated by a process of feedback.

The alimentary chain is ironically described in the verses of the Yorkshire folk song "On Ilkley Moor Baht' At":

---

[4] Joseph Campbell, *The Way of the Animal Powers: Historical Atlas of World Mythology,* vol. 1, p. 47.
[5] *Theogony,* lines 116ff.
[6] *Gaia: A New Look at Life on Earth,* p. 22.

> Tha'll go an' get tha deeath o' cowld . . .
> Then we shall ha' to bury thee. . .
> Then t'worms'll come an' ate thee oop . . .
> Then t'ducks'll come an' ate oop t'worms . . .
> Then we shall go an' eat oop t'ducks . . .
> Then we shall all 'ave etten thee . . .

This reality appears to lurk behind the title of William Burroughs's savagely humorous novel *The Naked Lunch*. "The title means exactly what the words say: NAKED lunch—a frozen moment when everyone sees what is on the end of every fork."[7]

The mythographer Joseph Campbell describes this cyclic process in the context of a Sumerian terra-cotta plaque which depicts a lion-headed eagle biting into the rump of a beatifically smiling bull:

> It is the vision represented in our plaque of the lunar bull and solar lion-bird; but it is represented on the plane of earth as well: by the living bull and lion who in Mother Nature's heart dwell in everlasting peace, even now, as they enact their monstrous mystery play of life, which is called "Now You Eat Me!"[8]

In the midst of the devouring and destruction the mistress of all life is at peace with herself. Predator and prey are part of the same image, the same environment, belong together. An apocryphal story tells how herring in a zoo's aquarium failed to thrive and breed, despite all the efforts of the skilled staff, until one zoologist had the bright idea of introducing the herrings' natural predator, the dogfish, whereupon the herring colony became healthy and viable.

In the ecosystem of our dreams we sometimes have glimpses of our inner nature feeding on itself: an alligator snaps up a fish, a tortoise gobbles down a slippery reptile; a more highly charged psychic element is always ready to assimilate a weaker one. A cat, proud, playful, sure of itself, is pounced on and devoured by a tiger, portraying a moment when more house-trained pleasure-loving instincts are lost to a wilder surge from the deep, dark psychic jungle, a force that won't tolerate strokes and blandishments.

---

[7] *The Naked Lunch,* p. v.
[8] *The Masks of God: Occidental Mythology,* p. 58.

The uroboric process in which one form gives way to another, in the psyche as in the physical world, may be thought of as existing prior to any divine marriage or sexual embrace. The following lines are from the Upanishads, but we might also hear in them the voice of the self-devouring Mercurial serpent of the alchemists:

> I am the food of life, and I am he who eats the
> food of life: I am the two in ONE.
> I am the first-born of the world of truth, born
> before the gods, born in the center of immortality.
> I am that food which eats the eater of food. I
> have gone beyond the universe.[9]

In like vein, in the apocryphal Acts of St. John, Christ sings from the center of a round dance, "I will eat and I will be eaten."[10]

As Erich Neumann says,[11] the visceral needs precede the sexual, both ontogenetically, in the primacy of the oral stage, and in terms of the evolution of species, since asexually reproducing entities existed long before the emergence of the two sexes. Jung writes:

> *Hunger,* as a characteristic expression of the instinct of self-preser-
> vation, is without doubt one of the primary and most powerful fac-
> tors in influencing behaviour; in fact, the lives of primitives are
> more strongly affected by it than by sexuality. At this level, hunger
> is the alpha and omega—existence itself.[12]

The great round, the beginningless and endless cycle of existence, has often presented itself to the human imagination in the guise of the Great Mother, producing, feeding and devouring the myriad forms of life. The mother archetype has a particularly intimate connection with food imagery. Mother (Latin *mater,* Greek *meter)* is cognate with matter (Latin *materia),* and as Earth Mother (Gaia) she provides the literal substance of food (all substance be-

---

[9] *The Upanishads,* pp. 111f.

[10] See Jung, "Transformation Symbolism in the Mass," *Psychology and Religion,* CW 11, par. 415.

[11] *The Origins and History of Consciousness,* p. 27.

[12] "Psychological Factors in Human Behaviour," *The Structure and Dynamics of the Psyche,* CW8, par. 237.

ing potentially food) and with it a very basic metaphor which recurs in our speech and in our dreams in association with all areas of life. She feeds and sustains with the milk of her breasts, so often emphasized in her ancient images. All nutrition comes from the great *nutrix* or wet nurse, who holds the child to that life-sustaining breast and imbues it with a sense of secure being. To sustain means to hold from underneath; a woman who touched this feeling of security as if for the first time, while walking in a park, reported, "I felt as if the earth was holding me up." The Earth Mother is the giver of fruits and grain, and mistress of edible animal life, enabling us to go on being and to grow into ourselves. Mother is the one who feeds us before we have a separate identity, and it is against the background of her that that separate identity evolves, along with our sense of inner and outer, as we take in what she provides.

To that same *nutrix* belongs also the bad breast which deprives and starves us by withholding or secretly taking back; in one woman's dream mother was associated with a tapeworm, a hidden robber that lives in the depth of the gut. She also devours us, as we recognize in the hideous grin of certain Aztec statues, or in the blood-drinking images of Kali with tongue hanging out and threatening tusks, or the Tantric goddess Vajravarahi ("Diamond Sow") with her skull-cup. She is the witch who feeds the lost children with tasty gingerbread before starving Gretel and fattening up Hansel for her own dinner. She feeds us, but we must feed her. She takes on many theriomorphic forms such as the "gently smiling" crocodile, or tigress, with large mouth and the "masculine" attribute of powerful teeth ("all the better to eat you with"). Under grandmother's reassuring bonnet gape her wolfish jaws. Distressed mothers of some species literally eat their young; the negative mother complex swallows our capacity to live as individuals.

In the mother complex, the network of associations that attach to the notion of "mother," images of the archetypal (or Great) mother are interwoven with those of the personal mother, and in the metaphorical language of dreams images of food frequently cluster about this figure. Gardens in which the good earth yields up cabbages, carrots, leeks and potatoes, and trees heavy with ripe fruit announce her presence. Cauldrons steaming with soups and stews, fragrant apple pie and bread fresh from the oven are her handiwork. The kitchen or dining table are among her favourite venues.

The following fragments of an analysis illustrate the interplay of food imagery and mother. During a lengthy period of therapy in her late thirties and early forties, Jennifer, a separated woman with a young daughter, struggled with the many ramifications of a negative mother complex. Her unconscious identification with her mother was signaled by an early dream in which mother and daughter go into a cake shop together. Mother buys Jennifer a birthday cake, but to the dreamer's annoyance it has her mother's name written on it in icing sugar. The feeding and devouring aspects of mother are both contained in this image, for in offering this supposed treat the mother complex proposes to assimilate the daughter. The price of the cake (as threatened in the Hansel and Gretel story) is the dreamer's individual identity. On the day which should celebrate her birth as a separate being it is announced (sweetly, in icing sugar) that she is once again drawn back into identification with mother.

The same dream began with Jennifer driving her mother's car, and innumerable other dreams took place "in my mother's house." The woman who had brought Jennifer into the world had a very destructive and controlling masculine side which, in the language of one of her dreams, flattened people like a heavy old flat-iron; it had squashed Jennifer's self-confidence and sought to keep men firmly pressed down. She had been dissatisfied with her marriage and had several affairs before it finally broke up. She had ended up an alcoholic, and it was disturbing to contemplate her as the model for Jennifer's own life.

When a child is difficult with food this may be an expression of dissatisfaction with the psychological food the mother offers. The little Jennifer had been picky, and was allergic to milk, though this was not realized at the time. During her work with me, dreams several times brought back the memory of how grimy her mother's kitchen and cooker used to be—an unappetizing environment. As an adult she was rather overconcerned about diet, forever looking to food to provide the elusive sense of well-being that the good mother imparts, while at the same time wishing to keep the size and shape of her body firmly under control, wanting desperately not to resemble her mother physically. Since mother is associated with matter, mother problems are inclined to be reflected one way or another at the level of body and body image, and are frequently concretized in eating problems.

Raw food diets were a great favorite of Jennifer's, food straight from the larder of bountiful nature herself, ready to eat. Salads and fruit also featured in her dreams, notably in association with the transference. In the first such dream I offered her salad and we sat and ate together. Another dream went as follows:

> I am on my way to see Eve, walking from the underground station. I pick fruit from trees laden with huge William pears and avocados. Then I get home and start to prepare them. X is there too, preparing food, and asks where I got them from. I say, "round the corner," and she says they are expensive. I see X has bacon on her plate and I feel guilty. I say, "but there are nuts if you prefer." X tells me it's okay to eat meat occasionally, then turns to me looking stern and says, "when I was a child we only had meat on special occasions."

Jennifer's work with me was bringing her into contact with the good mother whose fruits hung ripe and ready for plucking. The avocado, Jennifer had read, was full of concentrated nutrients. William pears were juicy but *messy*. Taking a pill prescribed by a doctor is a clean operation, but working with the psyche is messy, and to get at the juice one must be willing to get one's hands dirty.

Fruit is often associated with goddesses of fertility and maternity and the pear was sacred to Isis and Hera. The dream fruit had to be taken home to be prepared for assimilation, taken to the personal center of Jennifer's life and made her own. Here a slightly more critical attitude comes in, in the guise of X, an older woman who, significantly, had cured herself of a serious illness through dietary therapy. X is a model of a successful cure, and also something of a mother figure. She reminded Jennifer a little of her maternal grandmother (which of course means great mother) by whom, despite a difficult relationship with Jennifer's mother, another link in the chain of family neurosis, Jennifer had felt loved as a child. "She was stern, but she cared for us more than my mother. She used to feed me after school, make my favorite food for me." Pears had also put Jennifer in mind of this grandmother. X points out that Jennifer is paying a lot for this fruit. Though plucked straight from the tree it is in the context of the therapeutic process which has to be paid for—and not only with money, but with honest effort too.

Then, in the midst of this raw vegetarian food, there is the bacon. At the literal level X, whose word obviously counts, gives permission for a less rigid attitude to diet, but by eating the bacon she is also demonstrating, as one who knows about the curative properties of food, the assimilation into consciousness of the mother complex as pig, that is at the level of instinct, of animal dependency.

The pig, despised as "unclean" by societies who fought to displace her worship, was widely considered sacred to mother goddesses. The pig taught humans to turn up the earth, was the first plow, hence associated with cultivation and the Greek corn goddess Demeter. The sow nursing her large litters of piglets, fleshy and hairless like human babies, symbolizes fertility and abundance, but is also said to be inclined to consume her own offspring.

In one story the Egyptian sky goddess Nut assumes the form of a pig and eats her children, the stars, to give birth to them again in the morning. The Yuletide boar's head, with the goddess's apple in its mouth, is no doubt related to the Roman sacrifice of a pig to Ceres, the Roman equivalent to Demeter, during the Saturnalia festival, a variant of which also continued under the Byzantine church as a Christmas pork feast following the fast of Advent. In the context of the Eleusinian mysteries, sacred to Demeter and her daughter Persephone, the pig was on one occasion at least referred to as *delphax,* womb animal.[13] A pregnant sow was often sacrificed to Demeter,

---

[13] In Epicharmus, quoted in C. Kerényi, "Kore," in Jung and Kerényi, *Introduction to a Science of Mythology,* p. 165.

and piglets, embodiments of the corn spirit, were thrown into a chasm during the Eleusinian rites in honor of the divine mother and daughter. Many myths also tell of the boar, the destructive masculine aspect or consort of a mother goddess.

In the dream X points out, as it were, that there are different forms of mother, different aspects to be assimilated. The dreamer had no sense of guilt at what could have been seen as the theft of the fruit. It was innocent fruit picking, as if taking place before the Fall. But this experience of paradise is not enough. The process that starts with taking the fruit leads on to the confrontation with the guilt-producing meat, a theme to be explored more fully in the next chapter, for the sterner side of nature pushes us to grow out of our childish notions of innocence and see how we are implicated in the often destructive processes of life. The moment when a child comprehends the relationship between animal and meat often brings revulsion. It is linked to the development of conscience, that is, the consciousness of the consequences of our actions. However guilt, like bacon, is unhealthy if one overindulges in it. Perhaps, too, the "special occasions" referred to are those feasts at which the otherwise taboo meat of the sacred animal may be eaten for purposes of ritual assimilation.

The motif of being fed by and of feeding the analyst is a common one in dreams, often with maternal implications. That the analyst should provide food for the analysand is an obvious notion, but unless the process is to be stuck in an infantile dependency the reverse is also true. The analyst too must be nourished by the process, otherwise there is boredom and staleness. Also, the analysand must be able to experience giving. Reciprocity and feedback are essential to keep the process alive, and mother must be found within, not just projected onto the person of the analyst. Dreams of providing the analyst with food are often an encouraging sign that the analysand feels she has resources, something to give, and that there is an exchange of psychic energy. On the other hand, one client dreamt early in the therapeutic relationship that he brought his own packed lunch to eat at my house. He did not stay long in therapy as he did not want to risk the diet I might have had to offer. He wanted to take in only what he had come prepared with and for, so there was no way for the new to enter.

The longing for the good mother can transform itself into cravings for all kinds of substitutes. Jennifer sometimes ate compulsively, sometimes drank unwisely, but above all she sought to fill her inner longing through sex, as her mother had done through alcohol and very likely sex as well. Jennifer parted from her husband shortly after her work with me began, and continued an affair which had been going on for some time. In this as in later entanglements, her neediness constantly got in the way of her capacity to see the destructiveness of her behavior. She wanted to feel looked after. She wanted sex. Being on her own was intolerable. With the help of a few glasses of wine to "send the guards to sleep," she would end up in bed with the man she'd sworn to separate from, or for that matter with any convenient and inappropriate male body, to lapse into depression and self-disgust afterward.

During the long-drawn-out agonies of trying to finalize the ending of the relationship with the first lover, she dreamt:

> Stephen has come back in the night, but it is light. He gets into bed with me. I use something like breakfast cereal as a contraceptive, pushing it into my vagina.

She was beginning to see (though night, it was light) that her sexual craving was in part a longing for the comforting embrace of mother, the provider of cereals. The dream image contrasts with the Freudian expectation that instinctual activity is displaced upwards from the sexual organs: here the nutritive instinct is displaced downwards. Her sexuality has become devouring. With the dreamer's increased understanding a new day is hinted at (breakfast), but the compulsive feeding of her sexual parts is blocking the possible birth of something new.

At one point when she thought she had finished with Stephen, Jennifer dreamt that when walking with two small children she met a milkman at a crossroads. The mention of milk, the primary maternal feed, evoked the negative association of her allergic reaction. But her milk is carried by a male figure, who is met at a crossroads. In mythology the lord of crossroads was Hermes, the tricky god who could travel in all directions, and surely it was he whom the dreamer met. His androgyny, that is his ability to slither from "masculine" discrimination to "feminine" relatedness is expressed in his milkman role. The god of lies then points back down the road along which she has come, and tells her it is not advisable to go that way; it is a long, cold road, especially for children.

As in so many myths and fairy tales, where there is one door you must not open, or one fruit you must not eat, Jennifer, naturally, chooses the road back. Eventually she comes to a pub she has been to with Stephen. Here she steals some bulbs from the garden to take home and plant for blooms in future years. Then she comes to a shop. The theft, the shop, both again tell us we are in the dubious business world of Hermes-Mercury, god of the market place, messenger, fleet of wing and foot. There was psychic movement, but it was paradoxical movement. Consciously Jennifer was struggling to put the relationship with Stephen behind her, but something tricky was going on, and she found herself drawn back for a considerable time into this place of cold comfort and little obvious support for the developing aspects of the psyche personified as children. But buried there were prerequisites for future growth and choice.

Jennifer's complaint about Stephen was that he was never there for her, always letting her down by failing to turn up when he said he would, absenting himself and frustrating her needs. This source of irritation appeared to be standard among women in her maternal line: even if the man was physically present he was emotionally absent (her mother's complaint)—escaping, no doubt the best way he could, from a demanding, controlling woman. Dreams hinted that this destructive pattern was associated with many who had gone before, and that it fell to Jennifer to take on the task of washing the family laundry. No wonder she had to go back again and again into "my mother's house," where so often in her dreams she found herself in bed with Stephen. The relationship was a battle for power, a war often waged in the bedroom. Demonstrations of love would be followed by retreat and rejection, and wounded feelings would lead to anger and retaliation. Jennifer would withdraw after lovemaking, "needing to be alone." Stephen would repair to the golf course.

The neediness can be understood causally, as a natural response to maternal deprivation, but to look at the problem as causal and linear is to lose the whole picture, in which longing and devouring and depriving are all present all the time.

The most destructive psychic component manifested itself repeatedly in dreams of vampires and werewolves. When the good mother absents herself, the destructive maternal animus, her inferior masculine side, readily steps in to fill the gap, his tearing tusks or canine teeth eager for business. In one of Jennifer's dreams he appeared as a boar, consort of the sow mother, goring a young woman, but several times he came in wolfish guise, and repeatedly as Dracula.

Jennifer had early confessed to a fascination with vampire stories, and relished the peculiar frisson produced by the mixture of demonic power and sexuality. Embodying passionate desire without relatedness, the fanged demon lover regularly visited her, his lust for blood draining away the libido from her feminine ego. Dracula should be long since dead. He is buried, entombed, out of sight and out of mind. But he rises from the depths of the subterranean unconscious, always at night, when the light of consciousness is weak, to enslave and destroy. Blood is the food the shades of the dead require in order to participate in the world of the living, and this diet demands that the living give up some at least of their vital substance. Those whom the vampire feasts on become themselves vampires, and when Dracula assaulted Jennifer she became vampiristic, devouring, greedy for the blood of men. From her conscious point of view it was simply that she had needs which required quite reasonably to be met.

Slowly her resistance to these attacks increased and the vampire figures began to lose their power and become more manageable. It was similar with the werewolf dreams. Like the vampire, the werewolf operates at night, coming not from underground but in perverted form from the dark forest of our untamed animal nature. Dracula had a particular association with wolves.

On the same night she had the milkman dream, Jennifer dreamt:

> I am with a man in, or wanting, a relationship with him. Then there is a well, and a wolf is down it. The question is how to catch it. They send down two small children. When they bring them up the wolf follows. Two men cut him open. As they cut into the liver and kidneys, liquid comes out and he starts to transform into a man. I ask if they are going to sew him up again, and they say no, this would be wrong.

This dream marked the beginning of the real analytical process. The dreamer senses the possibility of a relationship with an unknown man, her true inner partner. Again the two children feature (their sex was unclear), and again they are put in some danger, more so than in the milkman dream. It is as if the psyche insists on the fact that what has been unfolding and growing must be risked now if the real work is to be done. The unfinished business of the relationship with Stephen was the material out of which consciousness could grow. The wolf must be lured out into the daylight and painfully humanized.

The helpful inner man now appears in the guise of the two surgeons. Their sharp knives, unlike the wolf's teeth, can be used in a healing and positively transformative way. The expression of fluids, of symbolic bile and of many literal tears, was an essential part of the process. Jennifer often wished the long operation could be brought to an end, and the wounds speedily sewn up, but the process could not be hastened. As the humanization of the wolf-mother-animus, of the vulpine desirousness proceeded, and she found in herself the nourishing qualities that enabled her to break out of the family pattern and truly take care of both herself and her own growing daughter, her compulsiveness gave way increasingly to newly-discovered creativity and unexpected contentedness. Now she had formed a good relationship with the inner man, and he seldom reverted to werewolf.

If a woman needs to exercise discrimination when mother offers food, it seems to be even more essential for the development of masculine consciousness to learn to say no. The Jewish mother jokes with their refrain of "Eat, eat, my boy!" convey a danger which is not confined to Jewish men. The following is the initial dream of a young man with cancer:

> I am in prison. My cell door is open, and through it I can see the condemned cell opposite. The warder goes into it, carrying a tray full of food for the condemned man, whom I don't actually see. I can see that he has a colour TV in there, too. I marvel at how the man can apparently enjoy these things when he is going to die tomorrow. The warder comes back and I bend to tie my shoelace so that he doesn't see me looking. He walks past.

The condemned man made the dreamer think of his father, sitting passively in front of the television while his wife brought him supper. The warder appears to be a controlling, masculine aspect of the mother, bearing her death-tainted food, and indeed the prison itself could be regarded as the imprisoning mother complex where the condemned man, the dreamer's unconscious passivity recognized only in projection in his father, is fed and entertained. The dreamer, though apparently free to leave, remains in his cell. He avoids confrontation with his jailer. In real life he was trying to combat his illness with a regimen of healthy living, but—whether or not this would have made a difference—lacked the self-discipline to give up his indulgences. The inadequate father-image was of no help in this respect. He died six months later.

The fairy story "The Raven" in Grimm's collection places particular emphasis on food in its account of the hero's journey to release the princess from her imprisonment in the form of a dark-plumed bird. If we read this story as an account of a struggle on the part of masculine consciousness to emancipate itself to the point where the inner marriage can take place (the story ends with the announcement of the wedding), the unconscious feminine element appears initially only as some sort of dark, gloomy intuition encountered in the shadowy forest. The hero is a generally passive figure who would get nowhere without constant promptings from the raven princess. His first task is to refuse the food and drink offered by an old woman in the forest. To partake of it will result in his falling asleep and missing the encounter with the princess, but despite the warning, when temptation comes he steps right in each time, three times in all, unable to resist taking a sip from the glass proffered by the old witch, with motherly coaxing, "Come on, just a little won't harm you . . ." Mother has so many little ways of keeping us unconscious. Of course in real life this might not come in the literal form of mother. It could be the boys in the pub: "Go on, have another one!" Anything rather than wake up to the task of becoming a man, leaving the kitchen for the great adventure: self-indulgence where resolution is needed.

Our hero, despite this abject failure, is nevertheless helped on his way by the persistence of the raven princess who is actively seeking to engage him in his task. Having failed to wake him by shaking him, she leaves him a loaf, a piece of meat and a bottle of wine. This food, far from sending him to sleep, will sustain him endlessly. However much he consumes it will never grow any less.

Here we run into a motif often found in fairy tales and folklore, that of the inexhaustible supply of food. It appears elsewhere in the image of the table that spreads itself, the magical porridge pot, the raven that feeds Elijah in the desert. It is the spontaneous flow of sustaining material from the unconscious. One of the terms used by the alchemists which corresponds to our concept of the unconscious was the *massa confusa*. The word *massa,* mass, is related to the Greek words *maza,* barley cake, and *massein,* to knead. The confused mass of unconscious psychic processes is kneaded into shapes we can assimilate, if we have the right attitude.

As this "food" is assimilated, so more becomes available, in this case more of the same basic fare, already processed and fashioned in the unconscious. The conscious "I" must still connect with the inner cornucopia before this can happen. A woman not yet able to do so dreamed repeatedly of restaurants with abundant food which for one reason or another she could not eat—the food would slip off her plate, or it was the wrong time of day—or of coming out of a vast supermarket with an empty trolley. Another, aware of an inner abundance she could not get access to spoke of the sensation of starving in a land of plenty. In "The Raven" there is no such problem. Eating the food represents movement toward consciousness, reversing the tendency of the old woman's food. The tireless impulse of the raven, working out of sight of the hero toward recognition and release, is sufficient to keep him going.

The primary attribute of mother is of course her capacity to give birth, and being devoured by her may, as in the case of Jonah, lead to rebirth, just as the solar Horus or Re at evening enters the mouth of the great sky cow Hathor or Nut to be born again at dawn. Regression to an infantile or embryonic state of consciousness may precede a new phase of growth. Nevertheless the maw of the Great Mother is always a threat from the point of view of consciousness. Nor is it only "mother" who threatens to swallow us. The voracious nature of unconscious forces is portrayed in widespread images, male and female, with gaping mouth and long canines. Sometimes it is Devouring Time in the form of the lion-headed Mithraic figure of Aion or flesh-eating Shiva Mahakala (Great Time) rather than female Kali, personifying the great oubliette into which memories fall, occasionally retrieved by heroic effort. *Tempus edax rerum,* time is the devourer of things.

To propitiate the dangerous forces of nature which can swallow up human life and consciousness, food is regularly offered to the gods and goddesses. The gods are more likely to look benignly on us if we relate to them, and tend to wreak their worst when ignored, deprived of our awareness. In his temple, Yahweh was fed a male lamb morning and evening, along with cereal offerings and libations, like an honored guest, quite apart from the food offered for ritual purposes by individuals. Whether a sacrifice is offered in the hope of receiving benefits, to ward off threatening powers, or in imitation of a divine act, it is an acknowledgment that in this world of perpetual transformations nothing is truly free, there is always a price to pay.

Food from father is different in nature from that of mother. Christ is the bread of heaven, spiritual food, the word of God the Father which we need for sustenance as much as the bread of the world. I once dreamt of finding a volume of Jung's collected works on a restaurant table, pointing archetypally to the realm of logos as a source of nourishment. Father, too, can be devouring: rigid and fearful old Cronus-Saturn eats the future potential of his children. A dream: "Father is eating people—they are just lumps. He says, 'They're dead anyway.' " A woman who had just had an encounter with her personal father, which had stirred up old feelings of worthlessness through her inability to live up to his expectations, dreamed of an eagle blocking out the light and swooping down "as if it was going to swallow me up." The eagle was the bird of sky-father Zeus. The dream was followed by a depression during which she spoke of losing her sense of self; it was overwhelmed by the father complex.

Many gods are associated or identified with particular foodstuffs, especially with those foods that are of vital importance to a culture. But it has also been explicit in certain traditions that we are food for the gods. The Maya Book of Counsel, the *Popol Vuh*, states that humans were made of maize:

> And the Forefathers, the Creators and Makers, who were called Tepeu and Gucumatz said: "The time of dawn has come, let the work be finished, and let those who are to nourish and sustain us appear, the noble sons, the civilized vassals; let man appear, humanity, on the face of the earth.". . .
>
> And thus they found the food, and this was what went into the flesh of created man, the made man; of this the blood of man was made. So the corn entered [into the formation of man] by the work of the Forefathers. . .
>
> And then grinding the yellow corn and the white corn, Xmucané made nine drinks, and from this food came the strength and the flesh, and with it they created the muscles and the strength of man. This the Forefathers did, Tepeu and Gucumatz, as they were called.
>
> After that they began to talk about the creation and the making of our first mother and father; of yellow corn and of white corn they made their flesh; of corn-meal dough they made the arms and the

legs of man. Only dough of corn meal went into the flesh of our first fathers, the four men, who were created.[14]

As tends to be the case with cereals in general, corn (in this context maize) to the old populations of America had maternal connotations. "American Indians, in their many different languages, always spoke of corn as 'Our Mother,' 'Our Life,' 'She Who Sustains Us.' "[15] To be made out of corn is therefore to be made out of mother's own substance, just as to be formed from clay is to be made of the substance of Mother Earth. The corn image, however, conveys in addition that we are food, food for the gods, thus making offerings to them is a way of preserving ourselves, for the time being at least, from being eaten.

Similar ideas were inherent in Aztec theology, uniting death and renewal, god and man. The gods had sacrificed themselves to create humanity, and humanity must reciprocate with human sacrifice in order that life continue. According to Lewis Spence,

> The gods . . . declared that war was necessary in order that blood might be obtained for the nourishment of the sun. . . . [This myth] reveals the whole theological idea at the center of Aztec faith: that man was created especially for the purpose of keeping the gods alive, that, indeed, he was nothing but a beast of sacrifice whose blood nourished the elemental powers, and this was his whole reason of being.[16]

In his commentary on a dream,[17] Jung interprets the phrase "to dine" as meaning "to eat the complexes"—a necessary part of the process of becoming more conscious. But our complexes eat us too—"like a maggot eating away at my life," said one tormented and frustrated man. "What's eating you?" we ask a person with an anguished look, or we speak of bitterness gnawing away at someone, or of being eaten up with jealousy or envy. The Yanomami of the Venezuelan forests express this experience in the belief that

---

[14] *Popol Vuh: The Sacred Book of the Ancient Quiché Maya*, pp. 165ff.

[15] See Margaret Visser, *Much Depends on Dinner*, p. 24.

[16] *The Religion of Ancient Mexico*, p. 49.

[17] *Dream Analysis*, p. 12.

demons eat souls.[18]

In connection with the word association experiment Jung refers to the "assimilating complex,"[19] which is always ready to draw new associations, to say nothing of conscious purposes, into its web, and behind our personal complexes live the gods, requiring tribute. The alchemical green lion that devours the sun, the natural and ferocious desirousness that eclipses consciousness, is one image of this process. The light-giving sun vanishes, and all that remains is desire.

What little consciousness we have may be dined on by archetypal forces over which we have no control, but making offerings is a more or less conscious act. Every time we offer something which belongs to us we are giving a little of ourselves, sacrificing a bit of ego attachment. Honoring that which is greater, making a small act of submission, places us in a certain relationship to the gods. Rendering thanks, as when saying grace at mealtime, also keeps us aware of this relationship.

Returning for a moment to "The Raven," on receipt of his new food supply the hero becomes more active; he sets off to find the princess and dares to enter the house of a giant. Giants are well known for their tendency to eat people, and he saves himself from this fate by offering the giant, and subsequently his brother, food from the inexhaustible supply, whereupon the giants help him, with maps, to find his way. Offering food to placate these brutish, subhuman elements involves no real sacrifice on the hero's part—there is more where it came from—but it involves quick-wittedness in a dangerous situation, making use of the resources that have been spontaneously presenting themselves, and which he has in the meantime been assimilating. He is learning from experience.

To feed an animal can be an important component in taming it. Small children readily learn to hand out food to ducks, squirrels, horses, as a way of relating to and befriending these foreign

---

[18] Jacques Lizot, *Tales of the Yanomami: Daily Life in the Venezuelan Forest,* pp. 124ff.
[19] "A Review of the Complex Theory," *The Structure and Dynamics of the Psyche,* CW 8, par. 197.

species. Feeding the giant means giving it substance, affirming its reality, taking it seriously and gaining its cooperation. The word "body" is related to the Sanskrit *bandha,* of which the primary meaning is bondage or fetter; the body is envisioned as binding the soul. Feeding, giving body to the psychic image, binds it to us just as an act of hospitality carries with it a bond or obligation. By relating to the giant in this way the hero acknowledges the existence of this crude psychic component. Instead of being overwhelmed and absorbed into its archaic mode of functioning, the hero gains more points of reference in the inner landscape.

In the Jataka tales of the Buddha's past lives it is related how the Buddha as the prince Mahasattva cuts his own throat in order to offer himself as food to a starving tigress and her cubs. The Tibetan Chod meditation practice, ideally done in a cemetery, involves visualizing oneself being eaten as an experience of the relative nature of the ego. All psychic components can increase or decrease in strength, and in so doing assimilate one another. To realize this constitutes an illuminating moment in which the underlying unity is glimpsed, and the "I" becomes less important.

The experience of being devoured is a common feature of shamanistic initiation. The future shaman is torn from his ordinary ego standpoint by transpersonal powers and embarks upon a journey into psychic realms, an experience which enables him subsequently to act as healer and guide of souls. A Tungus shaman from central Asia, interviewed in 1925, gave the following account of his initiatory illness at the age of fifteen:

> After that, my ancestors began to shamanize with me. They stood me up like a block of wood and shot at me with their bows until I lost consciousness. They cut up my flesh, separated my bones, counted them, and ate my flesh raw. . . . The same thing happens to every Tungus shaman. Only after his shaman ancestors have cut up his body and separated his bones can he begin to shamanize.[20]

In this experience the initiate ceases to be an individual; he is pared

---

[20] Quoted in Campbell, *The Way of the Animal Powers,* p. 172.

back to his separate bones, the imperishable components of his being, and assimilated to the ancestral, archetypal shaman.

The conscious self-sacrifice of Prince Mahasattva to the devouring mother tiger unconscious is followed in due course by a new birth. In Christianity too, the self-sacrifice of the divine being, his descent into the maw of death and his resurrection, is the central image, and it is ritually celebrated in a ceremony which involves eating. In "Transformation Symbolism in the Mass" Jung comments in depth on the Christian communion. "In so far as Christ is both sacrificer and sacrificed, there is a mystical unity of all parts of the sacrificial act." He compares the imagery of the mass with the vision of the third-century C.E. alchemist Zosimos of Panopolis, whose sacrificial feast "consists in his tearing himself to pieces with his own teeth and eating himself." Jung continues: "This recalls the saying of St. John Chrysostom that in the Eucharist Christ drinks his own blood. By the same token, one might add, he eats his own flesh."[21] Christ is often envisioned in edible terms, as the bread of heaven, the sacrificial lamb, the fish, the first fruit, the vine/wine and the hidden manna.

In devouring raw animal flesh, the followers of Dionysus seem also to have been eating their god, though this may not have been always explicit.[22] The followers of Christ confront and consume the terrible image of torn flesh in a more distanced way, eating his mutilated body which is at one and the same time the bread of human achievement, the raw suffering of incarnation, the divine life essence and the wine of ecstasy. Of related meaning is the totem meal, in which the sacred animal, embodying the spirit of the clan, in turn becomes embodied in the clan members, its flesh being transformed into their flesh, signifying the integration into each individual of all that the totem represents. In the *unio mystica* of the sacrificial meal the communicants take in, and thereby attempt consciously to experience, their own divine nature.

---

[21] *Psychology and Religion*, CW 11, pars. 337, 346, 353.
[22] Ibid., par. 353, note 25; also Walter Otto, *Dionysos: Myth and Cult*, p. 131.

da's highly specialized diet of a certain kind of bamboo is a major reason for its near extinction, and the creodonts, once the dominant group of carnivores on this planet, are thought to have become extinct some thirty-five million years ago because their teeth were too exclusively designed for meat eating. A person on a strict diet, or with a narrow conception of what constitutes food, makes a poor traveler. To eat whatever comes one's way implies flexibility and openness to new experience. Speaking of the need to develop a robust, accepting attitude to life, a Zen master said:

> Look at the canary bird. It is tiny and weak and doesn't live long. And what does it eat? Just seeds. On the other hand, look at the pig, which is big and strong and has a long life. What does the pig eat? Everything. We must be like the pig, we must eat everything.[27]

In the process of enlarging consciousness this is the proper attitude. When it comes to assimilating unconscious contents we cannot afford to be too fussy, but must take what comes. Omnivorousness means variety, of what goes into the mouth, of the type of place where individual foodstuffs are found, and of the techniques required for obtaining them. It involves willingness to learn and allows room for creativity. Our ancestors needed not only a very tolerant digestive system, but curiosity and a readiness to experiment, like the seagulls who feed off inland rubbish tips, and the nutritionally adventurous rat. In other words they needed a capacity to learn quickly, to take in new things metaphorically as well as literally.

Animals with more specialized eating habits need only be programmed to respond to the right kind of food (the caterpillar of the monarch butterfly recognizes only milkweed as dinner, the cat will pounce on any small creature that squeaks and runs about), whereas the non-specialist has to learn, from experience and especially from elders, just what is edible. A herd of goats, under natural conditions, is led on foraging expeditions by an old nanny, who guides them along a route carefully chosen to fill the animals' various dietary requirements.

---

[27] Suzuki, c. 1968. Personal communication from D. Stevens.

In humans a drive toward exploration and a well-developed capacity for handing on knowledge are concomitants of our highly variable eating pattern. Over the millennia, and according to the diverse geographical regions where necessity has driven us, we have constantly had to adjust to changes in habitat and economic circumstances, now focusing on particular foodstuffs, now diversifying, and our lifestyles, along with many of our myths and collective rituals, as well as our language, have changed with our diet. Necessity, curiosity and cultural tradition dictate what we eat more than instinct does, and our eating patterns connect us to our environment, as societies and as individuals, in a particular way. At one time the word meat, meaning food in general, came to be applied to flesh, for that was considered the basic food. At another, bread has been considered central, "our daily bread." The two strands of hunting and gathering continue to combine and separate.

The Fruit of Paradise

The myth of the exit from the forest to the savanna is strong in contrast, evoking an age of peaceful browsing with apparently little bloodshed followed by one of great savagery and daring. This is of course the simplified version, but it is at home in the popular imagination of those who have a degree of knowledge of evolutionary theory. It is remarkable how the story of these ancestors in the forest, for whom food simply grew on trees, a theory which emerged in the nineteenth century, has a distinct flavor of the original paradise, that garden of plenty without tears or labor. It seems that in the archetypal imagination the intuition or memory of preconscious wholeness appears to us clad in the fruit-bedecked greenery which was once home for our prehuman ancestors. Primates are essentially frugivorous. Perhaps too the place where the fruit trees grew was often beloved of the nomadic hunter-gatherer as a welcoming, restful place to return to, calming the soul.

There are of course two kinds of paradise, the original "home," the source of our deepest nostalgia, and the paradise to be attained one day, after painful struggle, by the faithful, the brave, the good or the wise. The word itself comes from the Persian for a walled garden. In the teachings of Zoroaster it described the nature of the world before evil entered it, and as it would be again after evil was overcome. The original paradise is usually envisioned on earth, that of future reward is often of a heavenly nature, but this *alpha* and *omega* overlap in their imagery, as if the attainment of the paradise hoped for in the future is paradoxically a kind of return.

Hesiod relates that during the Golden Age of the past, "the fruitful earth unforced bare [men] fruit[28] abundantly and without stint," and that the Greek heroes of the Trojan war "live untouched by sorrow in the islands of the blessed along the shore of deep swirling Ocean, happy heroes for whom the grain-giving earth bears honey-sweet fruit flourishing thrice a year."[29] Fruit is to be found in both places, but apparently not meat.

In the garden of Eden "made the Lord God to grow every tree that is pleasant to the sight, and good for food. . . . And the Lord God commanded the man, saying, Of every tree of the garden thou mayest freely eat." (Gen. 2:9, 2:16)[30] Again no mention is made of animal food. Of the Biblical paradise to come, a similar impression is given of nonviolence in matters of food:

> The wolf also shall dwell with the lamb, and the leopard shall lie down with the kid; and the calf and the young lion and the fatling together; and a little child shall lead them.
> And the cow and the bear shall feed; their young ones shall lie down together: and the lion shall eat straw like the ox. (Isa. 11:6-7)

In the Koran, the paradise for the Mohammedan faithful, with its emphasis on sensual pleasures and cultural attributes (silken robes, couches, silver vessels) is only once mentioned as providing meat, and then it is fowl, a more, as it were, spiritualized form of flesh. For the most part the emphasis is again on fruit, along with drinks flavored with ginger and rivers flowing with incorruptible water, milk, honey and wine.

---

[28] In Greek the word *karpos* included grain in addition to what we call fruit.

[29] *Works and Days,* lines 117-118 and 172-173.

[30] Biblical references throughout are to the Authorized (King James) Version.

On thrones decorated, Reclining on them. . . . Round about them
shall go youths never altering in age, with goblets and ewers and a
cup of pure drink. . . . And fruits such as they choose. . . . And ba-
nana-trees (with fruits), one above the other. . . . And abundant fruit.
. . . And the fruits of the two gardens shall be within reach. . . . And
for them therein are all fruits and protection from their Lord. . . .
And its fruits shall be made near (to them), being easy to reach.[31]

It is said in Islamic tradition that when the believers in paradise
eat the fruit of the lotus tree they no longer yearn for earthly life;
also that God sent the angel Ridhwan to earth with a celestial apple
for Moses when his hour had come, and that so enraptured was
Moses by the scent of this apple that he gladly abandoned his body
and followed Ridhwan.

It is fitting that food should come without killing in a place of
deathlessness. "They shall not hurt nor destroy in all my holy
mountain." (Isa. 11:9) In the case of Hesiod's Golden Age death
came eventually, but it was like going to sleep, a nonviolent death.
Porphyry was explicit in his belief that in those good old golden
days people were satisfied with grass, leaves and acorns, which
could be plucked wild, and the killing of animals came later, together with war, as also did cultivation and work,[32] a view which
has elements in common with our current science-based understanding of prehistory.

The taking of life tends to be associated with guilt and fear of
retribution, emotions out of place in paradise. It is a most ancient
and widespread practice to ask forgiveness of the animal hunted
down and even of the plant uprooted, or in some way ritually to de-
flect blame. In Greek sacrifices the victim had to be seen to
"assent" to its slaughter.[33] Fruit on the other hand is designed by
nature to be eaten, to the purpose that the seed within, discarded, or
passing through the alimentary canal and eliminated whole, will

---

[31] *The Qur'an*, 56, 55, 47, 76.

[32] *On Abstinence from Animal Food*, pp. 65f., 146ff.

[33] See Marcel Detienne and Jean-Pierre Vernant, *The Cuisine of Sacrifice Among
the Greeks*, p. 9.

thus find a suitable site to grow.

> If we omitted to gather them, [the plants] would spontaneously drop
> their fruits. The gathering of fruits, also, is not attended with the de-
> struction of the plants, as it is when animals lose their animating
> principle.[34]

Fruit is thus the most innocently edible substance. It may also be
picked wild and is often eaten raw, therefore its consumption does
not necessarily involve laborious processes. A ripe fruit invites
plucking and eating and promises immediate satisfaction, without
effort or conflict.

It may be that while men hunted it was women, the gatherers,
who tended the fruit trees. At all events the paradisical garden with
its fruit was anciently ruled by a goddess.[35] Examples are Nemesis,
in her capacity of goddess of the sacred grove, and especially
Aphrodite, addressed here in a poem by Sappho:

> Hither to me from Crete, to this holy temple, where is
> your pleasant grove of apple-trees . . .
> Therein cold water babbles through apple-branches, and
> the place is all shadowy with roses.[36]

Apples were regarded as an appropriate offering for the love
goddess. The golden apples of the Hesperides (the three daughters
of Evening) grew on a tree presented by Gaia to Hera as a wedding
gift, presumably to endow the blessing of fruitfulness. Eve, too,
mother of all beings, must once have been such a mistress of the divine orchard. In ancient Italy there was a fruit goddess known as
Pomona, who took as her lover a mysterious god called Vertumnus
of Tuscan origin, associated by the Romans with the turning year,
making this a union of seasonal fertility. Their story is told by Ovid
in his *Metamorphoses*. In the Sumerian garden of the gods sits
Siduri, the lady of the vine and maker of wine. It is said, too, that

---

[34] Porphyry, *On Abstinence from Animal Food,* p. 71.

[35] See Robert Graves and Raphael Patai, *Hebrew Myths: The Book of Genesis,* p.
80.

[36] D. Page, trans., *Sappho and Alcaeus,* p. 34.

the apple, fig and grape were gifts of Dionysus, who spans the domain of fertility from wild nature to arboriculture and viticulture and ecstasy-inducing wine.

The term "apple" is not here a botanical definition. Various species hide behind the apple myths. In a number of modern European languages as in ancient Greek, the word could be used to refer to any large roundish fruit. This extended meaning is reflected in such coinings as the English pineapple (French *pomme de pin),* "love apple," the original English term for the tomato, the Italian *pomadoro* (tomato) and the French *pomme de terre* (potato). Aphrodite's "apple" may well have been the quince. In the case of the Biblical "apple" the choice of translation may have been influenced by the coincidence in Latin of two forms of the word *malum,* one meaning "bad, evil," and the other "apple." In Jewish tradition it has been speculated that the fruit of the tree of knowledge was a fig. The apple of myth is the *summum bonum* of the frugivorous, tree-dwelling primate, a big, round, desirable fruit shining among the leaves, promising sweetness.

The word "fruit" comes from the Latin verb *fruor,* meaning "to have at one's disposal, to have the enjoyment of," and so "to enjoy, find pleasure in, delight in."

The plump, moist fruit of the apple goddess embodies fertility, sensuality, sexuality, pleasure, desire. It was an ancient custom for Athenian couples to share an apple on entering the bridal chamber as Zeus and Hera might have done to enjoy Gaia's wedding gift. According to Ad de Vries, "In many parts of Europe trees are made fruitful by giving its *[sic]* first fruit to a pregnant woman."[37] As the tree feeds her, so, in a sense, is she to feed some of her fertility to the tree. She will thus develop a relationship to the tree, and it will represent something growing in her own psyche to which she directs psychic energy. The tree of her life is encouraged to prosper, she who is also a fruit bearing a seed. Nana, nymph mother of Attis, conceives by putting a ripe almond or pomegranate in her bosom; it

---

[37] *Dictionary of Symbols and Imagery,* under the entry "Fruit."

was from the tree which sprang from the severed male genitals of the androgynous Agditis (Cybele). Persephone's loss of her girlish innocence is sealed by eating a pomegranate seed given her by Hades. Less sweet than apple or pomegranate, but passionately red, the tomato, alias love-apple, sometimes fruits in modern dreams to hint at love. In the Song of Solomon (2:3-5) we read:

> As the apple tree among the trees of the wood, so is my beloved among the sons. I sat down under his shadow with great delight, and his fruit was sweet to my taste.
>
> He brought me to the banqueting house, and his banner over me was love.
>
> Stay me with flagons, comfort me with apples: for I am sick of love.

The following dream came to Zoe, who had been through a long and often painful analytical process. She had repeatedly been swept away by states of rage, despair and fear of abandonment. Slowly these had abated as she found a firmer standpoint, and life had become far more manageable. She missed, however, the old intensity she had experienced when she was less reflective and feared that life might remain rather dreary.

> I was sitting against a tree, weeping. I was in a forest that had been destroyed by fire, amidst the scorched remains of blackened tree trunks and charred stumps.
>
> A tinkling laugh wafted toward me and I caught a glimpse of the Wild Woman skipping barefoot through the dead wood. I made after her. As I drew near she hid behind a tree, to re-emerge then disappear again. Playfully weaving her way through the forest, she teased me to follow, darting back and forth in and out of view, laughing the while—enticing me on.
>
> We came to a clearing filled with light where a magnificent fig tree stood: lush green leaves spread wide on branches bowed with fruit poised ripe and full. Wild Woman plucked a fig. She ate slowly, intent, with succulent relish, juices trickling down her chin— a feast of sensual delight.

The Wild Woman, the natural woman inimical to patriarchal values, had been a recurrent figure in her dreams, free in spirit and associated with the moon, but she had shown a frightening side earlier, a violent rage when the dreamer was unable or unwilling to relate to her. Now the dreamer's attitude has shifted, allowing the wild woman to become initiator and guide, showing the way playfully to the tree of life in its eternal fruitfulness and demonstrating the juicy sweetness that is within reach. Among trees the fig is especially abundant, producing fruit four times a year under the right conditions. I thought of another passage in the Song of Solomon:

> For, lo, the winter is past, the rain is over and gone;
>   The flowers appear on the earth; the time of the singing of birds
> is come, and the voice of the turtle is heard in our land;
>   The fig tree putteth forth her green figs . . . (2:11-13)

Zoe recalled being in the South African bush with a friend who had remarked that it was time for a forest fire; it was needed for renewed growth. The dream forest has been blackened by the raging fires of emotion, burning off the dross and cleansing in the heat of the alchemical *calcinatio* and now, when all around seems black and the dreamer laments, in the midst of her tears the sound of laughter draws her on to see in the light the greenness *(viriditas)* and fruitiness of the apparently indestructible tree.

In the well-known tale of Snow White, the life-giving fruit woman is given a darker cast as the wicked stepmother. When the witch mother comes to entice Snow White, now living with the seven dwarfs, to her doom, she takes the form of an old woman peddling deceptively attractive wares. She comes three times, and each time Snow White is conned into buying an item that looks appealing but is devastating in its effect. The third and most powerful is the poisoned apple. From the outside it looks so lovely, white with a red cheek, that whoever saw it would long for it, but whoever ate it would be bound to die. In fact it is the red side that is poisonous, and to overcome Snow White's apprehensions the wicked queen cuts the apple in half and eats the white half herself. Snow White bites into the red half; the piece of poisoned apple lodges in her throat and she falls into a deathly coma. She is laid to rest in a glass coffin, to be awoken later from her deathlike sleep by the prince.

The apple Snow White finds irresistible has a profound and universal appeal. It is full of the natural sweetness of life; it is like Snow White herself, the whiteness of innocence tinged with the blush of passion. One taste of passionate desire and the coma sets in. In the development of feminine consciousness, when the link to the positive mother is missing, contact with life in all its fullness is tentative, fearful and lacks the guidance of good instinct.

What happens to Snow White happens to many a young woman. Naive and flushed with ardent longing for love she reaches out toward an unsuitable object. The trouble is that she is unable to distinguish between that eros which springs from the soul's need to journey forward into a relationship of equal partners, and the regressive yearning for mother love, with its dependence on the partner. Her desire is bound to be thwarted. Her passion is too full of disappointment to bear. It sticks in her throat, indigestible, and paralyzes her, cutting her off from the world as if by a sheet of glass. The prospect of being hurt again is too terrifying; she prefers to feel nothing. It is only after a long period of dormancy, no longer even tempted to seek what she desires or even to know it, that processes working away in the unconscious, personified in the story as the prince, draw her back into life, free at last from the baneful influence of the negative mother.

In Greek mythology the story is told of Atalanta who grew up under the protection of the virgin goddess Artemis. She has been told that she will never be happy in marriage, and declares that she will only marry the man who outruns her, in the belief that none can do so. Aphrodite, well known for her dislike of celibacy, gives one of Atalanta's suitors, Hippomenes, three golden apples, which he throws into her path during the race. Atalanta stoops to pick up the apples. Hippomenes overtakes her, her Artemis-inspired attachment to eternal tomboyhood is overcome, and she is enticed into relationship, though her brief happiness is terminated by the fulfillment of the prediction.

Another fruit connected with Aphrodite and, like the apple, associated both with fertility and with the pleasures of sexuality, is the peach. According to the English herbalist Nicholas Culpeper it inclines the eater to lasciviousness. The seventeenth-century English poet Andrew Marvell conveys in his poem "The Garden" something of that divinely sensual orchard where the goddess's bounty is freely available:

> What wondrous life is this I lead!
> Ripe apples drop about my head;
> The luscious clusters of the vine
> Upon my mouth do crush their wine;
> The nectarine, and curious peach,
> Into my hands themselves do reach.[38]

In contrast to this fruity bliss, Tantalus is tormented in Tartaros with branches laden with apples, pears, pomegranates, figs and olives, always just out of reach; his hell is an inverse paradise.

Fruit similes are common in erotic descriptions of the female body, smooth and curvaceous, rounded and firm or fleshy, luscious, juicy; breasts like peaches, mangos; apple cheeks, cherry lips; natural, wholesome, pleasure-giving, seductive, voluptuous. "Thy temples are like a piece of a pomegranate," "thy breasts [are like] to clusters of grapes." (Song of Sol. 4:3, 7:7) In the British imagination Nell Gwynne, with her basket of fruit and her plunging neckline, has become iconic, a dish to tempt a king: "Come buy my sweet oranges!" Saint Augustine equated original sin with sexuality because of the frightening autonomy of sexual arousal, and because sex is the biological means of transmission of life and characteristics from generation to generation, but the pagan associations of the apple no doubt also contributed to this formulation. Thus Christianity opposed the values of the spirit to the natural and sensual; the erotic, the aphrodisiac became the forbidden fruit.

The goddess's garden, that happy valley of dreams where fruit freely offers itself, can, as I have suggested, be a dangerous place. It finds its echo in the medieval legend of the Land of Cockayne, of which there are numerous versions, where the houses are made of

---

[38] *Selected Poems*, p. 42.

barley sugar and cakes, or herrings and ham, the streets paved with pastry, and animals turn themselves on spits. This of course is not a natural paradise but a fantastic environment of culturally sophisticated goodies, a fantasy born of hunger, to compensate for the looming presence of the Terrible Mother—or a place of dependency, to cling to which is to avoid the task of developing consciousness. The gingerbread house with sugar windows of the Hansel and Gretel story, which takes place against a background of famine, echoes the Land of Cockayne, as does a song of the 1950s by Burl Ives, "The Big Rock Candy Mountain":

> Oh the buzzing of the bees
> In the cigarette trees
> The soda water fountain,
> Where the lemonade springs
> And the bluebird sings
> On the big rock candy mountain!

It is an image of eternal childhood, of gain without pain.

But the apple is also the fruit which, as the gift of a goddess, endows immortality for hard-won heroic achievements, for poetic skills and for wisdom. This is why one of the tasks of Heracles is to steal some of Hera's apples from the garden of the Hesperides. Given to the sacred king, the apple or apple branch ensured his entry into Elysium. Robert Graves suggests that etymologically the name Elysian Fields originally signified apple orchards,[39] and this is certainly the case with Avalon, the apple tree paradise to which the mortally wounded King Arthur was taken, and whose resident goddess was Morgan. Avalon is a version of the Irish paradise Emain Abhlach (Emain of the Apple Trees), an island where grows a great tree that bears fruit and blossom at the same time.

The apple is the fruit of the tree of eternal life or, in the Nordic myths of the goddess Idun, the food which maintains the eternal youth of the gods. The fruit of eternity is often clad with the incorruptibility of gold.

---

[39] *The White Goddess*, p. 254.

In Egyptian mythology the fruit of immortality was the fig or date, dispensed from the tree of life by Hathor or Nut as Lady of the Date Palm to regenerate the dead. In China similar symbolism attaches to the peach, which is the emblem of marriage and symbol of immortality and springtime. The peach tree whose fruit endows immortality grows in the gardens of the goddess Hsi Wang Mu, the Royal Lady of the West, who dwells on the K'un Lun mountains, sometimes identified with Mount Sumeru, the center of the universe. The peach is an important ingredient in the elixir of immortality of the Taoist alchemists, and the god of longevity is often pictured emerging from a peach. Protective powers are attributed to peach-wood and peach-stones, amulets being made out of them.[40] It is also said that on one of the Chinese Islands of the Blest the saints partake of mulberries, and the rowanberry and hazel nut are also fruits of immortality in the Celtic tradition.

Alchemists often likened their mysterious work, which Jung identified with the individuation process, to a tree. The fruit of the tree corresponded to the work's goal, the Philosophers' Stone or true gold, in one case imaged as the radiant sun hanging in the tree like a golden apple.[41]

The primordial paradise is not wild nature, but a garden, originally a walled garden, an inner space, where nature is wedded to order, at peace with herself, tended by unseen hands. The opposites are held in balance, nothing is excessive or discordant; it is the state of equilibrium that existed before our chaos and may one day exist again, when we have learned to tend our own inner garden. In the Golden Age there was no split between nature and culture; the land naturally produced foods that were as if cultivated. Fruit is the end product of the growth process, maturity, the fullness of time ("by their fruits shall ye know them"), and at the same time contains the new seed. The roundness of the apple indicates the completeness of

---

[40] See C.A.S. Williams, *Outlines of Chinese Symbolism and Art Motives;* entries "Peach" and "Hsi Wang Mu."

[41] See Jung, "The Philosophical Tree," *Alchemical Studies,* CW13, esp. par. 404.

the beginning and the completeness of the end, the perfect sphere of the One. A round fruit in dreams may represent what Jung calls the Self in all its nourishing naturalness, an image of our wholeness.

A woman dreamed that at last she left the parental home, with all that implied in terms of freeing herself from the power of inherited hang-ups and the distorting imprints of her upbringing, and of coming into her own; she was carrying with her a melon, full of refreshment for the soul and seeds of future potential. For a woman the lady of the orchard may also be a fruit-giving image of the Self. Inquiring of the psyche what she needed in order to sort out her tangled life, a woman suffering from painful drivenness received the image: "I sit down on the grass in a garden, and a woman comes and offers me strawberries."

The end is in the beginning, and the beginning in the end, but in between lies the whole of human endeavor, which involves expulsion from the garden. To try to return to it by regression is to renounce the god-sent (or goddess- or serpent-sent) labor of conscious evolution. It is to be tied to the skirts of mother, whose food can poison or send to sleep. But the goddess of the orchard is also the inspiratrix, mind opener, initiator who leads the hero on, promising the divine marriage after many trials, nourishing certain aims and ideals; she is Eve, who leads Adam into the knowledge of good and evil, splitting apart the original unconscious unity. Conflicts arising out of desire produce consciousness, setting us at odds with the natural order. After the ingestion of *this* apple there is no such thing as a free lunch, but through all the lonely struggle the hero may glimpse again her hand holding out the apple, golden with the light of consciousness.

The sweet fruit—apple, peach, fig, grape—is divine life force in all its joyfulness; love, consummation, the lure of the soul, the promise of the divine marriage and the ultimate goal and reward. The fruit of the tree of knowledge or immortality transforms radically, and the Genesis story emphasizes that *eating* it is the decisive factor; the eating is the initiation. What has been outside is now inside; it has crossed the threshold of the lips and become incorporated. Eternity—or discrimination and conflict—is assimilated, embodied. In the one case Adam and Eve become more human through their new awareness; in the other the hero embraces eternity and heroic consciousness returns to the Self. In both cases the eater's substance is irrevocably changed.

We envision paradise with its fruits as existing in the mythical past or after wearisome life is over, but in its radiant readiness a ripe fruit is full of immediacy, of nowness, impressing on us, if we can understand, that paradise could be nearer than we think, perhaps just within reach.

> A traveler realized that he was being stalked by a tiger. He ran and ran, with the tiger behind him, and just as he could go no farther he came to a precipice. He threw himself over the edge, holding onto some roots, hoping to make his way down. Looking down, to his great distress, he saw another tiger, looking up at him. As he clung to the roots, praying that one of the tigers would give up and go away, he saw that two mice, a black mouse and a white, were gnawing at the roots he was hanging from. Just then he noticed a ripe strawberry growing close by him. He reached out for it and ate it. It was delicious.[42]

Meat, Power and Pain

Leaving the garden, or the forest, let us now emerge onto the open plain and contemplate the fruit of the great hunt. Meat has an altogether different quality from vegetable matter, a kind of intensity, the power of muscular animal life seized in the heat of the chase. The word "meaty" signifies something concentrated, essence without superfluous padding.

> Most gatherer-hunters are particularly excited when meat comes into camp, because, as they very readily tell you, "it tastes good." But perhaps the reason runs deeper, having something to do with the spirit of life meat once had, and which plants lack.
>
> Significantly, chimps also consume their occasional meaty meals in a way quite different from their normal eating habits. An observer at the Gombe Stream Reserve once saw a group of chimps spend the

---

[42] Zen story, source unknown.

whole day engaged in the business of sharing and eating the body of an infant monkey that could not have weighed more than a few pounds. This kind of disproportionate attention to meat eating is usual among our simian cousins.[43]

There has been much speculation about the links between meat eating, tool use, hunting skills, increased brain size and intelligence. Certainly the development of new skills to meet the demands of a new food source was a hugely important factor in human evolution. Fruit trees stand still, but large animals had to be outwitted by strategy where power of muscle, tooth and claw were lacking.

Elaine Morgan has emphasized in *The Descent of Woman* that the history of "man the hunter" refers essentially to the male of the species. If fruit has certain feminine overtones (garden, goddess, love, mother as place of origin), meat has masculine associations, especially red meat ("real men don't eat quiche"). Male muscle power is beefcake, high protein. In hunter-gatherer societies the men by and large do the hunting and the women concentrate on gathering, which allows them to keep the children by them. Young children could obviously be an impediment on a hunting trip, and might also be endangered, and their long period of immaturity makes each child a big investment.

For our nearest relatives, the chimpanzees, hunting is also primarily a male concern, though females do occasionally join a hunting party. From the days of the Paleolithic cave paintings when the horned god ruled the hunt, to the Scottish grouse moors where businessmen pay for the privilege of participating, it is *men* we see out there, with stick, spear, bow and arrow or gun. Among the Mbuti pygmies of the Ituri forest,

> A fond father will make a tiny bow for his son, and arrows of soft wood and with blunt points. He may also give him a strip of hunting net. The mother will delight herself and her daughter by weaving a miniature carrying basket.[44]

---

[43] Richard Leakey and Roger Lewin, *People of the Lake: Man, His Origins, Nature and Future*, p. 199.
[44] Colin Turnbull, *The Forest People*, p. 114.

There is also a strong connection between hunting and warfare, that other traditionally male preserve, similarity in the need for physical prowess and muscularity, the use of weapons, joint expeditions, coordinated and disciplined operations, the excitement of risk taking and blood lust. Hunting is often seen as a training ground for war. The pursuit of goals, of particular importance in masculine psychology, had a long-term training ground in the chase and hunting.

Meat feeds the hero, gives him something to get his teeth into. Throughout *The Iliad,* whenever the warriors eat, it is roast meat they tuck into. When, for example, Patroclus, at Achilles' command, lays out food before Odysseus and Ajax, it is "the backs of a sheep, a fat goat and the chine of a great hog rich in lard,"[45] which Achilles then joints, cuts up and spits. Occasionally bread is also mentioned, and on one occasion (book 11) the aged Nestor and wounded Machaon restore themselves with a pottage, otherwise only meat eating is referred to. At one point Agamemnon, leader of the Greek army, goads his men with the words,

> What of the idle boasts you made that time in Lemnos as you gorged yourselves on the beef of straight-horned cattle and drank from bowls brimful of wine?[46]

Valor and boasts of valor go with heroic, carnivorous appetite. Athenaeus, second-century C.E. author of *Deipnosophistae (The Learned Banquet),* opines that the reason Homer's heroes eat only meat is that the cleaning and preparation of fish was a complex and mainly female task, unsuitable for heroes. Exploits in the battle for Troy are frequently described in metaphors of the chase:

> Menelaus . . . was like a lion retreating from a farmyard when he is tired of pitting himself against the dogs and men, who have stayed awake all night to save the fattest of their heifers from his maw. In his hunger for meat, he has charged them, but without success.[47]

---

[45] Homer, *The Iliad,* book 9, p. 114.

[46] Ibid., book 8, p. 151.

[47] Ibid., book 17, p. 333.

The Trojans now stormed the ship like flesh-eating lions.[48]

As a hound who has started a fawn from its mountain lair . . . the swift Achilles . . . .[49]

Massimo Montanari in his book *The Culture of Food* describes the emphasis on fighting, hunting and the consumption of heroic quantities of meat as a significant feature of the northern tribes who became dominant forces in Europe after the collapse of the Roman empire. The degree to which these activities were valued in themselves among the Germanic peoples is illustrated by the equivalent in their mythology of the peaceful Elysian Fields of the Greeks and the Avalon of the Celts. In Valhalla, the hall of the slain, the dead heroes await the day when they will join the gods in their fight against the forces of destruction at Ragnarok, when the gods' dominion is doomed to end. They spend their days in the afterlife fighting and hacking each other to pieces, before returning to feast on the flesh of the boar Saehrimnir, who is slaughtered and cooked daily and restored each night. It seems that in this society the heroic struggle was an end in itself, a task never completed, with no return to tranquillity envisaged, no celestial orchard.

Muscular manpower and the heroism of war are still associated with a good appetite for meat. As I write this section a number of United Nations hostages have been released by the Bosnian Serbs. The first batch of men, the media felt it important to inform us, were greeted as returning heroes with a breakfast of steak, the second with a breakfast menu of "meat soup, roast veal, roast lamb and roast potatoes."

To hunt or go to war requires the self-reliant qualities of a man who has emancipated himself from mother. He is no longer a boy but a defender and provider who can "bring home the bacon." A man with dependency problems who had not successfully reached this stage and who looked to his wife (who normally did the shopping) to mother him, was reported by her frequently to bring back

---

[48] Ibid., book 15, p. 287.
[49] Ibid., book 22, p. 402.

meat from the market for her to cook, as if asking her to acknowledge his manliness.

The Grimm story of Iron Hans, which tells of the process by which masculine consciousness frees itself from the sapping influence of mother, shows the function and symbolism of hunting and meat eating in this struggle. At the age of two, Hans is out in the forest with his mother when they are seized by robbers and imprisoned in a cave. There they stay until Hans, still under twelve, challenges and defeats the robber with his club; the two return home with spoils from the robbers' den and are reunited with Hans's longed-for father. After rebuilding the family home with his father and learning to plow, Hans asks his father to procure him a walking stick and sets off on his own. In the forest he makes two giant-sized friends, whom he has first heard working in the forest, giving one the name Fir-twister, because he twists rope out of fir trees, and the other the name of Rock-splitter, because he breaks up rock to build with. The formidable trio set up house in a deserted castle, where Hans is attacked by a boar. He clubs it to death, and with his companions roasts it on a spit.

The three then agree that each day two of them should go hunting and one stay and cook the meat, nine pounds per man per day. While cooking, Fir-twister and Rock-splitter in turn are assailed by a dwarf who demands food from them; when food is denied the dwarf beats them up. When Hans takes his turn at cooking and is just skimming the pot the dwarf again appears. Hans twice accedes to the dwarf's demand and gives him some of the meat, but the third request he refuses. The dwarf attacks, but Hans fights back and sees the dwarf disappear down a hole.

The three companions return to this spot and Hans and his club are let down in a basket. The dwarf is guarding a chained princess. After killing the dwarf, Hans gets his friends to pull up the princess in the basket. Hans himself is to follow but, mistrustful, he substitutes the club for himself. The other two let it drop, whereupon Hans takes a ring from the finger of the dead dwarf by means of which he is able to summon air spirits, who tell him of his former friends' location. With the aid of the spirits he catches up with them on a boat, clubs his comrades, throws them in the water, takes the princess home and marries her.

The opening of the story describes a typical situation in which the boy, imprisoned in the mother complex (the cave/womb of the earth) serves the robbers (of his independently disposable psychic energy) until he rebels against this inner constraint and establishes a constructive, working relationship with his father and develops further skills. Then he moves into a more self-reliant phase, aided by the stick which embodies much-needed fatherly authority and by the rude force of his club, primitive tool of masculine power. Now new, valuable capacities emerge from the dark of the untamed forest of the unconscious, personified as Fir-twister and Rock-splitter, who can combine and separate what nature offers so as to convert them to deliberately contrived uses. At first he becomes aware of their presence by picking up sounds of activity. Eventually he sees them, finds out what they are up to and the value of it, and gives them names.

Naming confers power; when we are but dimly aware of some tendency and cannot name it, it is much harder to come to grips with. The conscious personality (Hans) is increased by taking on these additional powers of purposeful activity—but as it turns out they are only partly under conscious control and revert to behaving autonomously toward the end of the story. The qualities that had worked for him then turn against him and have to be subdued.

Just as Hans is beginning to establish his independence, he is attacked by the boar, which threatens to end his adventures prematurely. The boar is the aggressive male aspect of the natural, instinctual pig mother. It poses a deadly threat to heroic consciousness which seeks to wrest some autonomy for itself and break the bonds of instinct.

The widespread motif of the boar hunt is explored in depth by John Layard in *A Celtic Quest*, a powerful analysis of the story of Culhwch and Olwen. The boar is "the image . . . of nature outraged at having to be transformed, female in origin but in male guise to indicate its wild destructiveness."[50] Attis, youthful lover of Cybele, and in some versions of his story Aphrodite's favorite, Adonis, both toy-boys of a goddess, are each gored to death by a wild boar and never become heroes. In Egyptian mythology Horus is attacked by the evil Seth in the guise of a boar (the aggression of Isis in her pig aspect) and prevails, but loses an eye. Among the successful boar slayers are Meleager, who kills the wild boar sent by the vengeful mistress of the forest, Artemis, to devastate the kingdom of Calydon, and Heracles, another wielder of the club, who captures the boar of Mount Erymanthus.

In the midst of the forest of dark, untamed nature, Hans and his companions find a deserted castle, a construction of masculine power from past generations, as if waiting for him. No doubt it is his presumption in occupying such a place that lays Hans open to the boar's attack. It is like the echo of a childhood interaction, when mother restrains her son's adventurousness, instinctively using a sharp tongue to keep him under control. "Look, mum, I'm the king of the castle!" "Get down at once, you silly boy!" A natural response, perhaps, to an unruly child, but necessary for the growing man to challenge. Insidious self-doubts make him vulnerable: "Can I live up to this? Perhaps I'd better go back home." The achievement of independent choice and responsibility is threatened.

After his first night in the castle Hans goes into the overgrown garden, now decayed to the point where its is scarcely different from the forest itself. He has yet to learn to tend the garden of his soul and the natural tangle of the unconscious prevails. Here the boar rushes to pierce him like the emasculating inner voice from nowhere which parrots deflating injunctions and undermining warnings from childhood. "Don't you dare!" or, "You'd better leave that alone, it's too big for you." Listen to that voice and you're done for; the boar's got you. But Hans strikes back immediately, whacking the boar dead with his sturdy self-made club. He overcomes the wild pig aggression with his own, reasserting control

---

[50] *A Celtic Quest,* p. 11.

over his destiny. Now he has earned the right to stay in the castle.

Hans carries the boar inside, roasts it and eats it with his companions (processing and digesting the experience). To the phallic aids of club and staff is added the spit as Hans graduates to metal technology. Assimilating the meat of the boar, the prize of his heroism, marks the transition to hunting on his own initiative. Calculation, organization and planning now play an important part.

This is where the disruptive fourth figure in the shape of the dwarf elbows his way into the threesome and demands an unearned share of the meat, the hunter's prize. The dwarf appears in the middle of the cooking process which is quiet, slow, introspective even—now we hear of a new implement, the cooking pot, signifying interiority, stirring things over. As a vessel it also has maternal connotations, making a new kind of contact with the nourishing good mother.

A woman who had started a university course and was getting carried away by ungrounded intellect had a dream in which she had left her ancestral cooking pot on the stove to burn. She goes out and is chased by a student resembling a man who has treated her violently in the past. She ends up in a cheap, dark café with him and a powerful politician. In discussing the dream she knew that the food in her pot, which came from where her family roots were, and was of a type used by her female ancestors, was more nourishing than that of the café. She needed to stick to the image of the pot, the stirring, to bring her back to her center and protect her from the violence and power-hunger of the intellectual inner man that threatened her, at the worst with rape, at best with someone else's cheap substitute for home-cooked, integrated sustenance.

Unknown to Hans, trouble has been brewing. He is first confronted by it while skimming the pot. He has been stirring over the flesh of animal instinct and is now doing some separating out, differentiating, when he is confronted by the dwarf, who we subsequently learn to be a dangerous, malicious shadow figure who has been hidden away underground. Like the hero of "The Raven" he wisely feeds this figure—but not too much. He gives it just enough flesh to bring it more into consciousness without bolstering its energy too much. Then again he has a fight on his hands.

What is this inferior element? It keeps the princess, the nonmaternal feminine component of a man's psyche which Jung calls the anima, chained up in the unconscious, but also leads Hans to her and makes it possible for him to free and marry her. It is the anima who enables a man inwardly to make psychic connections with the unconscious and outwardly to form real relationships which are not based on his dependency needs. But he can only do this when he has overcome his longing to be mothered, found his own power, and also recognized that the exercise of will cannot achieve everything. Perhaps the dwarf represents some greedy, self-serving power-lust or aggressive sexual tendencies that must be conquered before relatedness can begin. As long as such tendencies are denied they cannot be confronted, but in feeding the dwarf Hans lends it some reality so that he can deal with it.

The killing of the dwarf also leads to control of the helpful air spirits, certain winged thoughts or intuitions which guide Hans to the princess. Up to this point the whole story has been very earthy, close to the meat-producing animal nature, but after the heroic challenge is met something more spiritual is released, without which, it appears, the marriage cannot be attained.

The theme of meat as the original goal of masculine search and its connection with liberation from the mother emerged in my work with Donald, an actor and writer who came into analysis after years of depression which prevented him from exercising his talents. He had enjoyed some early success, but as soon as he ran into rejections he seized up. His family had been poor and he had received little encouragement or recognition from his parents. He recalled that his mother had often beaten him when he was little, sometimes with a sadistic smile on her face. This nastiness had brought out his own sadistic side; as a child he remembered throwing stones at a neighbor's cringing dog, and this drama played itself out intrapsychically in the adult, with fantasies and dreams of a cruel, mocking man who taunted him for his cowardice.

Meat often cropped up in his dreams. In one which he had early in our work together, typical of a certain theme, he is in the army canteen, queuing up, hoping to find some kind of meat. When his turn comes there isn't any. He told me that he often dreamed about meat and particularly of being unable to get any. I mentioned that this search for meat put me in mind of man's role as hunter. He said, as if an important truth had dawned, "Do you mean I need to go and hunt my own meat?" Setting his mind on a goal and going after it steadfastly was precisely what he had difficulty doing. Needing to get away from home, at fifteen he had joined the army, a traditional route to manhood. As the dream indicated, he was still seeking the independence he had sought in the army.

In a later dream, Donald goes up to a restaurant counter and gets some meat. "I had three or four different types of steak on my plate, but each one of them turned into a thick, sloppy liquid, like brown custard." This dream came a few days after he had completed a significant piece of writing, the first for a long time. It had required a heroic effort to overcome the resistance of negative inner forces, but scarcely had he proved himself in this way than his solid achievement was being pulped again by the old devaluing tendencies, unwilling to allow him to enjoy his achievement.

The dividing up and apportioning of the carcass was originally the task of the hunter, who, on site, would cut out and consume the innards, the "pluck" or "guts." It may be that this is the origin of the use of these words to indicate the manly virtues of courage required by the effective hunter, who must be able to take calculated risks as well as deal the decisive blow.[51] The knife, essential tool of butchery, with its powers of penetration and separation is a potent masculine emblem. In existing hunter-gatherer societies it is generally the man deemed to have killed the prey who shares out the meat. Dividing up a large carcass poses particular problems, and the na-

---

[51] See Margaret Visser, *The Rituals of Dinner*, p. 228. R.B. Onians suggests another origin; since pluck originally meant the heart and lungs he derives the use from the identification of this part of the body as the seat of courage and "spirit." (*The Origins of European Thought*, p. 69)

ture of social divisions is closely tied to this process.[52] Invariably the portion a person receives depends on social rank, or on some deliberately devised egalitarian procedure. This same configuration of man, meat, apportioning and status is deeply embedded in Western culture. The Latin word for flesh or meat, *caro,* is related to the Umbrian *karu,* a part or portion and *kartu,* distribution.

Dividing into parts, separating this from that, is the process by which consciousness develops. The alchemists described this process as *separatio;* Jung called it differentiation.

On this theme, another of Donald's dreams culminated in a powerful image of carving up flesh. He is looking at a friend (John) who is practically submerged in the sea. Behind John stands a warrior, a samurai-like figure in a black robe. The dreamer suddenly knows he is about to witness an execution.

> John looked at me and gave me a silly big grin. It was pitiful. He didn't know that as he grinned the warrior was standing behind him with the tip of an unbelievably sharp knife only a fraction of an inch away from the exact center of his skull. The knife was held vertical to the top of John's skull with the warrior holding the handle in both hands, arms outstretched in front of him and slightly above his shoulder. He drove the tip of the knife straight through the center of John's skull, keeping the blade vertical at all times until it had journeyed some nine or ten inches through the center of his head.
>
> He levered the blade forward so it sliced through the center of his forehead and continued down the center of his face until he had severed the chin. He then pulled out the knife and placed the tip back at the center of John's skull keeping the blade vertical but with the edge at an adjacent angle to the original cut. Then he drove the knife down and levered it forward so that it completely severed the right side of John's head. (The front right quarter.) He'd done this almost exactly as one would expect someone to cut out the first wedge of a wedding cake.
>
> He continued on to cut out a number of smaller "wedges" of what was left of John's head and handed the pieces around to his subordinates, making sure to keep the original piece for himself. He then

---

[52] See Thomas Gibson, "Meat Sharing As a Political Ritual: Forms of Transaction Versus Modes of Subsistence," and James Woodburn, "Egalitarian Societies."

went on to raise his trophy in the air and use it to make a toast, after which everyone cheered and began to eat their prize.

John was, like Donald, an actor, and moreover greatly admired Donald's own talent. The head has always been regarded "as in a unique degree precious or holy, identified with the person and equated with that soul or principle of *life* which the *psyche* [in Greek] appears to be."[53] Among cannibals the head, especially of a strong and courageous man, has been particularly prized as conferring on the eater the qualities of the victim. Brain, like marrow, constitutes the vital essence. According to Plato the head was made round "in imitation of the spherical form of the All . . . it being the most divine part and reigning over all the parts within us."[54] In its roundness the head signifies wholeness, and here that whole is being divided up, with sharp, mathematical exactitude. Division into four, creating two pairs of opposites, is a universal motif depicting the process by which consciousness proceeds, sorting out this from that where once it was all one.

The sadistic shadow, which had haunted Donald's dreams and imagination, appears transformed into the initiator or sacrificial priest, commanding the power and precision of the warrior which Donald needs to find in himself, and at the same time demonstrating the value of taking apart "the actor," the one who borrows personae. The sharp blade is also the tool of the surgeon; the *tumi* of the ancient Moche culture of Peru was a sacrificial knife, which later evolved into a surgical knife used in particular by the Incas, and eventually became the emblem of the god of healing.

The ancient Greeks differentiated between slaughter of domesticated animals for sacrifice and consumption from hunting wild animals, which were not generally supposed to be eaten,[55] but at the altar it was again the men who wielded the knife and who distributed the meat in accordance with the male hierarchy. The only

---

[53] Onians, *Origins of European Thought*, p. 96.

[54] *Timaeus*, 44 D.

[55] See Marcel Detienne, "Culinary Practices and the Spirit of Sacrifice," in Detienne and Vernant, *Cuisine of Sacrifice Among the Greeks*.

exception appears to have been in certain rites which were exclusively for women. In the normal run of events women were only entitled to a share through their men folk, and correspondingly enjoyed lesser status. Women, like female chimpanzees, tend to eat less meat than their male counterparts. In *The Iliad,* perhaps because all warriors were deemed equal as comrades in battle, we read of meat being shared out in equal portions, but usually priests and those of high rank or special honor were given privileged cuts or quantities. Their portion was *geras,* a prize or reward, a mark of respect. Hector says to Diomedes that "the Danaan horsemen used to honour you with the best seat at table, the first cut off the joint, a never-empty cup."[56]

Heracles, after bringing the dog Cerberus from the underworld as one of his tasks, kills three of Eurystheus's sons in his outrage at being given a slave's portion of meat. (Perhaps Heracles, the lion-skin clad, requires the lion's share.) The Greek word for portion, *moira,* came to mean one's individual lot in life as meted out by the three *Moirai,* the Fates. The high price of best steak, which still implies manliness and status, reminds us of the great value placed on cattle in our history. To herd cattle you have to be tough (like the cowboy) and to own cattle on a large scale you have to be rich— unless you have the devious rustling skills of Hermes. In the ancient Mediterranean the chief currency was the cow, the first metal coinage consisted of bronze ingots in the shape of cowhides, image of wealth and status in a man's world, and the word "pecuniary" comes from the Latin *pecu,* meaning livestock.

The principle of apportioning meat according to status held until quite recently in European high society. A seventeenth-century guide to manners advises that it is important to know "what is the best piece, the piece of honour that must be served to the person of highest rank."[57] Carving the joint was, of course, an honor in itself

---

[56] *The Iliad,* book 8, p. 149.
[57] Antoine de Courtin, *Nouveau Traité de Civilité,* quoted in Norbert Elias, *The Civilizing Process: The History of Manners,* p. 119.

and a required social skill for gentlemen. It was generally performed by the master of the household or a distinguished guest, and carving at table survived into the middle of this century in Britain as the unquestioned task of the man of the house.

The Lion's Share
A Story from Somalia

The lion, the jackal, the wolf, and the hyena had a meeting and agreed that they would hunt together in one party and share equally among them whatever game they caught.

They went out and killed a camel. The four animals then discussed which one of them would divide the meat. The lion said, "Whoever divides the meat must know how to count."

Immediately the wolf volunteered, saying, "Indeed, I know how to count."

He began to divide the meat. He cut off four pieces of equal size and placed one before each of the hunters.

The lion was angered. He said, "Is this the way to count?" And he struck the wolf across the eyes, so that his eyes swelled up and he could not see.

The jackal said, "The wolf does not know how to count. I will divide the meat."

He cut three portions that were small and a fourth portion that was very large. The three small portions he placed before the hyena, the wolf, and himself. The large portion he put in front of the lion, who took his meat and went away.

Why was it necessary to give the lion such a large piece? the hyena said. "Our agreement was to divide and share equally. Where did you ever learn how to divide?"

"I learned from the wolf," the jackal answered.

"Wolf? How can anyone learn from the wolf? He is stupid," the hyena said.

"The jackal was right," the wolf said. "He knows how to count. Before, when my eyes were open, I did not see it. Now, though my eyes are wounded, I see it clearly."[58]

The proper apportioning of meat is at the heart of the Greek myth of the banquet at Mecone. In those days men and gods dined

---

[58] From Harold Courlander, *The King's Drum and Other African Stories.*

together; that is to say, humans had not yet developed consciousness of themselves as separate from the unconscious forces that
ruled their lives. The central character in this story is Prometheus,
the Titan, who has earlier sided with Zeus in the fight against
Cronus and has been taught useful arts by Athene. Prometheus, who
according to one story created the race of mankind, and whom Carl
Kerényi describes in a book of that name as "an archetypal image
of human existence," has befriended and championed humanity and
passed on his knowledge to these poor struggling creatures: "I
found them witless, and gave them the use of their wits and made
them masters of their minds."[59] He has even interceded on their behalf when Zeus in his wrath was about to destroy them.

At Mecone a dispute arises over the apportioning of the sacrificial bull, and Prometheus is called upon to arbitrate. He cuts up the
carcass and divides it into two portions, one consisting of the flesh
and innards and the other of bones cunningly covered with glisten-
ing fat—highly desirable in Greek eyes. Zeus is deceived into
choosing the latter, and in punishment withdraws his gift of fire
from men, condemning them to eat their meat raw. Prometheus
later steals fire from the gods on behalf of mankind. He is punished
by being chained to a rock where his liver is daily eaten away by an
eagle or vulture, and each night is renewed to be torn at again.

This division of the sacrificial animal into the gods' portion and
the human portion was the standard Greek practice. The (thigh)
bones belong to the gods because they are the enduring, "immortal"
part of the body and contain the marrow, the core of animal being.
The fat, volatilized into smoke, and the marrow, constitute the vital
essence of the animal, and are appropriate for immortals who live
on a subtle plane and therefore consume nectar and ambrosia, and
enjoy the insubstantial potency of incense smoke.[60] In this offering
a distinction is being made, but a connection also. By this voluntary
homage to the gods the humans seek to protect themselves against

---

[59] Aeschylus, *Prometheus Bound,* line 442.
[60] On this topic see Onians, *Origins of European Thought* , pp. 279ff.

the ever-present danger of being taken over by the powers the gods represent. From the point of view of consciousness, to dine with the gods looks rather like being devoured by them.

The humans consume the cooked meat. Marked off by their diet from the gods on the one hand, on the other they are distinguished from the animals, who eat their meat raw and in a lawless fashion, making no offerings to the gods.

> For the son of Cronos has ordained this law for men, that fishes and beasts and winged fowls should devour one another, for right is not in them; but to mankind he gave right which proves far the best.[61]

The *omophagia,* eating of raw flesh, practiced by the followers of Dionysus, deliberately destroyed this boundary, at least temporarily, reconnecting them with raw animal passion. Dionysus himself, in the Orphic myth, is eaten by the Titans *cooked,* which suggests that the Titanic consciousness which represses the Dionysian experience can assimilate it only in processed form.

The division of the meat is a manifestation of the process which is also expressed in Prometheus's instruction in the various arts and in his stolen gift of fire, the fire for cooking which is also the light of human consciousness, for "all consciousness separates."[62] The culture-bringer is a thief from the point of view of the mighty forces of the unconscious, and creates a vantage point from which we can see ourselves as other than the beasts, having a place to stand, albeit precariously, outside the pure impulse of instinct. To the Greeks the definition of the realm of the human, that is the conscious as opposed to the instinctual, as well as the status of individuals, was inextricably linked to sacrificial practice. Thus meat eating has been a hugely important determinant in our culture.

Another aspect of meat symbolism also appeared in Donald's dreams. Some time before he started analysis he had a dream that haunted him thereafter:

---

[61] Hesiod, *Works and Days*, lines 276-278.
[62] Jung, "The Meaning of Psychology for Modern Man," *Civilization in Transition,* CW 10, par. 304.

> I'm looking at a diesel engine with a big radiator. The engine is really working, shaking. Then meat starts to come out of the radiator, tons and tons of it. It smells half cooked with the heat of the engine.

This dream turned him off meat for some time. He told me the meat smelled like boiled mince. The shock of this image was the confrontation with the torn, bleeding substance of his animal nature, his suffering, mangled instinctual being which was numbed by depression. In us as in other species emotion is expressed in the body; we feel it in the rush of blood, palpitations, muscles clenching, trembling; our flesh embodies the raw experience. The Greek word for meat, *kreas,* is related to the Latin *crudus,* meaning bleeding or raw, and to the English "cruelty"; it connects us to "nature red in tooth and claw." In Donald's dream the meat is being processed in a crude, mechanical sort of way, which is faintly reminiscent of his mother's cooking, her way of preparing meat. The analysis offered a framework for further processing.

Pain and anguish are never far from the image of meat, as in the following extract from the dream of a woman who had distanced herself emotionally from distressing childhood experiences:

> There were a man and a woman, quite elderly and no one I recognized. They were in beds like a hospital in this place. They were my *parents*, this was definite. Also it was definite that I had killed them. But they were "alive" as all the other dead people were. They were in great pain and badly injured, and I could not understand why they were in pain if they were dead. The message was that the pain didn't end with death as I had thought it did.
>
> The man had only half a leg. The bottom part had been replaced by a metal rod and a sort of flat foot at the end. The other leg was all torn up and sort of rotting. The rest of him was all messed up too but it was less clear than the leg. His legs were lying on a sort of roasting tray with fat running about on it and what seemed to be burnt bits (like you get when you roast a joint). This was on top of the bed he was lying on.
>
> The woman was in a mess too. It was her legs that were particularly clear as well. They were both there but all ripped up somehow, and also on this sort of roasting tray. There seemed to be blood and some kind of running stuff, not quite pus but that sort of thing.

The dream graphically emphasizes the fact that we are made of the same stuff as the animals we eat, implying an overt or covert identification of killer and killed. In order to be a good hunter, in fact, one needs to be able to get inside the skin of one's prey. Among the South African Bushmen a hunter who has shot an eland with a poisoned dart will identify with it during the time it takes to die and will observe certain dietary and behavioral taboos.[63]

This deeply embedded knowledge that we survive at others' expense gives rise to an uneasy tension in the psyche. The spilling of blood implies guilt and fear of revenge; propitiatory rites surround the business of killing for food. The following practices have been reported in bear-eating communities:

> When the bear has been slain, it is usual to disclaim responsibility for his death. In northern Siberia today, the Ostyaks, Votyaks, Koryaks, Kamchadals, Gilyaks, Yakuts, Yukaghir, and Tungus will say: "Grandfather, it wasn't I, it was the Russians, who made use of me, who killed you. I am sorry! Very sorry! Don't be angry with *me!*" On the other hand, the general practice in North America was to praise the bear and to explain the occasion. For example, the Abnaki would tell the animal frankly: "I have killed you because I need your skin for my coat and your flesh for my food. I have nothing else to live on." The Ottawa, north of Lake Huron, would flatter him and plead: "Do not leave with an evil thought against us because we have killed you. You have intelligence and can see for yourself that our children are starving. They love you. They wish you to enter into their bodies. Is it not a glorious thing to be eaten by the children of chiefs?[64]

The Bible lays down how to avoid blood guilt from slaughter:

> This is the thing which the Lord hath commanded, saying,
>   What man soever there be of the house of Israel, that killeth an ox, or lamb, or goat, or that killeth it out of the camp,
>   And bringeth it not unto the door of the tabernacle of the congregation, to offer an offering unto the Lord before the tabernacle of the

---

[63] Campbell, *The Way of the Animal Powers*, p. 90.
[64] A. Irving Hallowell, "Bear Ceremonialism in the Northern Hemisphere," quoted in ibid., p. 148.

Lord; blood shall be imputed unto that man; he hath shed blood; and
that man shall be cut off from among his people. . . .

For the life of the flesh is in the blood: and I have given it to you
upon the altar to make an atonement for your souls. (Lev. 17:2-4,
11)

Among the ancient Jews only ritually slaughtered meat was considered proper to eat. The animal's blood, the bearer of the mysterious quality of active animal life, was poured over the altar, returned
to God in symbolism similar to the offering of fat and marrow
bones by the Greeks to their gods. Modern Jewish slaughtering is
still based on these rules. In ancient Greece likewise all proper meat
for consumption was slaughtered in a sacrificial ritual and the gods
were offered their portion. Elaborate procedures ensured that the
sacrificial animal was seen to agree to its slaughter, and the knife
was hidden until the crucial moment came. When domesticated
animals are eaten, this means killing a creature one has cared for
and protected, which can produce a particular conflict and need for
assuaging ritual. "It is the communally enacted aggression and
shared guilt which creates solidarity."[65] The guilt and the ritual
both bear witness to a certain development of consciousness.

The following verse well conveys the feelings of guilt that lurk
around meat eating. It comes from a recent improvised dirge for a
pig on the Greek island of Tinos, where each family, according to
tradition, kills a pig annually in December. It was recited during the
festive pork meal following the slaughter:

Tell me what I have done to you.
Why have you killed me?
And soiled your hands with my blood?
Have you no children?
No heart?
For a long time I was fine, in my mud,
And never harmed anyone, poor thing.
I ate everything you gave me and you rewarded me with a stick.
I brought a lot of little ones into the world,

---

[65] Walter Burkert, *Greek Religion, Archaic and Classical,* p. 58.

I fed them with my milk. They grew big.
And instead of getting thanks from your lips you plunged me into
   my own blood.
You caught me early in the morning, spread my legs apart and
   slit my throat with a sharp knife.[66]

Grain and Culture

With our present concerns about "denatured" foods, and our related
vital need to renew contact with the wilder reaches of the psyche, it
is hard to put ourselves imaginatively in the position of the Greeks
and Romans, who saw the edible products of tamed nature, of nature subjugated by human effort, as the only proper food for humans. Hunting and gathering in the strict sense had become
marginalized as ways of acquiring food in the wake of the great
success of a society based on agriculture.

The Romans distinguished *ager,* cultivated land, from *saltus,*
wild nature, the territory that lay beyond the fragile boundary separating civilization from wilderness.[67] Domesticated animals, ritually slaughtered, and plants grown in worked fields, carried with
them reassuring images of human progress. Agriculture had notably
introduced into the human diet an abundance of vegetable sub-
stances high in starch which became energy-providing staples including, crucial for the evolution of European culture, the development in western Asia of grain cultivation. Wherever it spread it
was experienced as a great advance and a great blessing so that it
could be maintained in the Iran of Mazdaism, that "who sows
wheat, sows good."[68]

Culture is rooted in nature but distances us from nature, and the
gap between animal and human, which humans have strenuously
sought to maintain and define, is marked by such distinctions as
raw and cooked, wild and cultivated, and by the host of implements

---

[66] From Maria Yannissopoulou, *L'Expression des Relations Sociales dans le
Partage de la Nourriture au Village de Potamia.*
[67] See Massimo Montanari, *The Culture of Food,* p. 5.
[68] Natalie F. Joffe in Funk and Wagnalls, *Standard Dictionary of Folklore,
Mythology and Legend,* under the entry "Wheat."

and rituals which accompany the animal function of eating.

The first major development in food processing was the use of fire, some 500,000 years ago, though as far as we know it was not widely used for cooking until 30-40,000 years ago. Later, as in the story of Iron Hans, came the cooking pot, some 10,000 years ago.[69] The careful apportioning process, the offering, the cooking of the meat at Mecone, involved deliberate, organized postponement of gratification, restraint of instinct, time for reflection. In more distant times the weapon power of the hunters and their possession of the carcass automatically gave them power over its distribution, as any powerful carnivore would have first rights to the prey it caught. The Prometheus story bears witness to holy deliberation, a conscious making of distinctions, further developed in the subsequent dividing up of the once-whole carcass among the human diners.

The liberating power of mechanisms that distance us from instinctual compulsion has been illustrated in an experiment with two chimpanzees. They were trained to choose between two portions of candy, one larger than the other, and taught that whichever they chose would be given to the other chimp, the remaining portion being given to the selector. The instinct to go for the larger amount was so strong that both chimps found it almost impossible to do anything other than choose the larger portion, despite knowing that this meant losing it, until they were asked to point not directly at the food but at Roman numerals, which they had already learnt represented the different quantities of sweets. The numerals enabled the chimps to detach themselves sufficiently from their natural impulse to make an advantageous choice.[70]

The advent of agriculture, as well as providing us with a normally more stable food supply and creating a place to call home, took us further from the spontaneity of nature, instilling a sense of separateness from her and at the same time of collaboration with

---

[69] See Glynn L.I. Isaac and Jeanne M. Sept, "Long-Term History of the Human Diet," in *The Eating Disorders,* chap. 2.

[70] See Sarah Boysen and G.G. Berntson, "Responses to Quantity: Perceptual Versus Cognitive Mechanisms in Chimpanzees *(Pan Troglodytes)."*

her, binding us together in new forms of co-operation, creating new divisions of labor and social complexities. The very word "culture" means in the first place agriculture, from the Latin *ager,* a field and *colere,* to till, which comes from a presumed Indo-European root *kwel* meaning to move around. So culture is moving things (originally the earth) around as opposed to leaving them in their natural state; it is rearranging nature.

Very many myths of planting cultures involve the death of a divine being from whose remains the food plants grow. Often the figure who is reincarnated in the plants is first dismembered. One such story, from Ceram in the Moluccas, is told at length by Joseph Campbell in *Masks of God: Primitive Mythology.* In it the corpse of the semidivine maiden Hainuwele is cut up and buried and from these interred portions grow the tuberous plants that form the basic food of the people. Better known to us is Osiris, the god who, as a king on earth, brings cultivation (particularly of grain and vine) and civilization to the Egyptians. He is killed and dismembered by his hostile brother Seth, and the pieces of his body are scattered about the country. In *The Golden Bough,* J.G. Frazer gives examples from Africa, Europe, India and the Pacific of fertility rites involving the dismemberment of a sacrificial victim, and the scattering or burial of the individual pieces, enacting this mythical theme.

The image is of a being who has once been whole and undivided now broken up for purposes of future growth. Analogous to the dividing up of the carcass of the sacrificed animal, this mythologem reflects the psychological process by which our original unconscious wholeness is rent asunder as distinctions appear, with the inherent risk of fragmentation, and the need to reunite them at a new level. One of the most basic of such distinctions is "human" and "other," an identification with the "human" which separates us from our animal nature. Above all what makes us human is our ability to reflect, and this means separating ourselves from the objects of our reflection. If the image of the whole round fruit represents that original wholeness, cultivation mythology, like meat rituals, brings with it images of breaking apart.

A Chinese folk tale relates how at one time rice simply rolled across the countryside in a huge grain or ball, and all people had to do was to wait for it to come by and help themselves. One day, however, a villager was too lazy to take his turn at waiting for the rice to come, and the rice just rolled past. Realizing too late the seriousness of the situation, the man chased desperately after the rice and hit it with an axe, whereupon it shattered into a myriad tiny grains. After this the rice rolled no more, and people had to plant the individual grains in order to eat.[71]

The breaking apart of the original wholeness goes with work. After the fruit of the forbidden tree had split the psyche through the perception of good and evil, the Lord told Adam, "and thou shalt eat the herb of the field; in the sweat of thy face shalt thou eat bread." (Gen. 3:18-19) No wonder great weeping and wailing ritually attends the death of the Plant Spirit in its many cultural forms, this one being who dies to give birth to multiplicity. The more distinctions we make, the more responsibility rests upon us. In the context of the development of individual consciousness, such as happens in analysis, it is often hard to accept that, for example, if one is in a relationship that is not going too well, and given that this generally means wrongs on both sides, the onus to make changes is on the partner who has begun to see more clearly and distinguish some of the hitherto entangled projections. This means abandoning attempts to bully the partner into changing and concentrating on one's inner work.

Cultivation means active engagement with the natural processes, and it developed out of millennia of observing them: the cycle of bud—flower—fruit—seed, the relationship between the above-ground plant and the underground root system, the variables of soil type and of light and shade, the competition between plant species, the activity of insects in flowers. Wheat is a hybrid that came into being in western Asia through deliberate plant breeding, clearly the application of accumulated knowledge. What is more, after harvest-

---

[71] Told to the author, source unknown.

ing it still has to be threshed, winnowed, ground, sifted, mixed, fermented, kneaded and baked to make bread; in fact the cultivation of wheat was preceded by grain-grinding techniques.

Bread and wine, notes Jung, "represent a definite cultural achievement which is the fruit of attention, patience, industry, devotion and laborious toil."[72] Human beings have rightly prided themselves in this achievement, and used it to define humanity. The epithet Hesiod attaches to the human species is "bread-eating." Homer tells us that the gods (unlike men) "eat no bread," and repeatedly qualifies men as bread-eaters; he also speaks of barley as the "marrow of men."[73] In Bali rice may be addressed in terms otherwise used only for human beings, and is thought to have a soul similar to theirs. Now we can understand better why the Mayan myth tells us that men were made from maize flour;[74] it goes with essentially human accomplishment.

Where the use of such sophisticated foods is not used to define mankind as a whole, it frequently distinguishes the civilized man from the uncultured barbarian. Enkidu, the wild man of the Sumerian Epic of Gilgamesh, from the third millennium B.C.E., eats grass until he learns to eat bread and drink wine. To the Romans, barbarians were people who didn't eat bread; to the Chinese they are people who don't eat rice. In England, the noble lord and lady were originally loaf-ward and loaf-kneader, revered guardians of a highly-valued cultural tradition (though we now speak of "loafers" as idlers).

Given the cultural connotations of cereals, it is small wonder that each precious grain or product is widely treasured. My mother taught me it was wicked to burn (or throw away) bread. In Japan punishment in the afterworld awaits rice-wasters, and in Burma it is considered reprehensible to step on a grain of rice. A friend visiting

---

[72] "Transformation Symbolism in the Mass," *Psychology and Religion*, CW 11, par. 382.
[73] *Iliad*, book 5, p. 342; book 13, p. 322; *Odyssey*, book 8, p. 222; book 9, pp. 190f; book 2, p. 290 and book 20, p. 108.
[74] See above, pp. 25f.

Tunisia was reprimanded for dropping crumbs of millet. It is not just a question of "waste not, want not," but to treat discourteously such an embodiment of the divine, self-sacrificing provider, and of human endeavor, places one outside the bounds of civilization.

The following is the first part of a dream:

> I was in an airplane flying very close to the ground as if we were about to land. We were very close to the roof tops of the houses below when all of a sudden we took off back up in the air at a very sharp angle. I realized that there must have been another plane close by and we had to go back up to avoid crashing.
>
> Then we were all on the ground, somewhere on a busy street with lots of people and shops, and we were all feeling very relieved. I also realized that we were still in London and was surprised as I knew we had been in the air a long time and thought our destination had been New York.
>
> The street was thronging with people, and a few other women and myself were talking with an unknown older woman. She had baked a big doll/statue out of Rice Krispies and she was encouraging us to sample it. I also noticed that she had Rice Krispies all over her, and she may have been made of the cereal herself. I took a little piece out of the doll as I like baked Rice Krispies. When I looked up again, about to reach for another piece, she had gone.

This is another dream with a strong feeling of initiation about it, this time into women's mysteries. The dreamer, Claire, in her late thirties, had embarked on therapy when trying to withdraw from a relationship which was not what she really wanted, and she was beset by panicky feelings. She had been in therapy for quite some time when this dream came, and things had moved very slowly. The dream begins in the air. This height theme had featured in her dreams quite often: flying with or without an aircraft, being off the ground, living on top of a hill, climbing a crystal mountain. Flight, or rising above things, though it can give useful perspective and even a rapturous and inspiring view, is often a reaction to fear, fear of engagement with life in a concrete way, of making things real and facing the consequences, the risk of disappointment, of getting hurt, of being found wanting.

Claire had a younger brother, who as the only boy in the family had commanded a greater investment of interest and expectation from her parents, and an older sister who had a robust style of demanding and getting what she wanted. A shy, introverted child, often tearful in her early years, especially it seems after the birth of her brother, Claire had not been able to get enough in the way of attention and support. Her father, whom she had had great affection for and a degree of identification with, was away a lot and his life was not centered on the home. Her mother set Claire an example of what appeared to be a very limited and conventional life, dedicated to serving her often absent husband, and she seemed unable to relate much to Claire's feelings.

The main message Claire drew from her early life, though it remained unconscious for a very long time, was that she was not good enough, had something wrong with her, couldn't have what she wanted as other people could. The family tree revealed a pattern of passive women afraid to live their own lives, and this was working itself out in Claire's life too. The unvoiced fear of some basic inadequacy gnawed away at her so that each time she tentatively reached for something she wanted and failed to get, it seemed to confirm her doom, leading her to withdraw prematurely from the battle, or not to venture at all. She had many dream images corresponding to this inner paralysis, particularly of prone figures in death-like states, and occasional dreadful moments of freezing in waking life too, of being unable to speak or act.

When images of food came up in her dreams Claire usually did not get any, except when she stuffed cakes or chocolate pudding into her dream mouth in desperate compensation, craving sweetness. (Others concretize this image in compulsive eating.) At other times there were images of food that had gone bad: life stuff that had not been embraced, that had gone to waste, potential nourishment that hadn't been realized, hadn't been used to help her gain substance so she could fully occupy her space in life. She had one dream in which her mother had cooked a pot of one of her favorite kinds of food, but it was not for her.

To return to the dream, the dreamer starts off in the air, but coming down. Fear of a crash sends the plane up again in a sudden, sharp-angled panic, but eventually it manages to land. Claire told me that someone else was in control of the plane, presumably a man, the inner pilot who is so inclined to take off with her—he had also appeared as a dancing partner who danced her off the ground. When we get off the ground we are moving in the realm of the abstract as opposed to the concrete. This is often much more comfortable for us; we can view life with a certain detachment and avoid facing difficult realities. The pilot, however, does now bring her down safely, if bumpily, and into a busy street with shops. She has landed in a much frequented place, that is, the dream describes an experience common to the run of citified humanity, an everyday sort of state where there is plenty of movement, of to-ing and fro-ing. Shops are places of exchange; metaphorically they offer possibilities for investing psychic energy in something we want or need. The street is in London, which Claire considered home, rather than New York, which might have been more exciting, a place to escape to for a stimulating break. She is back in her habitual world.

In the midst of this familiar activity she finds herself in feminine company. The central figure is the woman with the curious doll. "She had Rice Krispies all over her, and she may have been made of the cereal herself." This mysterious figure is nothing less than a twentieth-century version of the great Grain Mother.

Claire recalled that her grandmother used to make cakes out of Rice Krispies, which she had enjoyed as a child. Many mythological figures cluster around the theme of cultivation in general and cereal growth in particular, but above all, far and wide, we find the Grain Mother in her various manifestations. For the Greeks she was Demeter, for the Romans, Ceres. Behind the civilizing figure of Osiris stands his sister-wife Isis, who discovered the wheat that Osiris cultivated. In Asia there are Rice Goddesses, in North and South America Corn (Maize) Mothers. The annually renewed plant growth tends to be identified with a young deity, often a maiden who is the youthful form of the Mother, sometimes a youth. Inherent to many of these stories is the theme of death and resurrection, of a journey to the underworld and a connection with the presiding deity of the realm of shadows.

The greater emphasis on female figures in these myths gives them a particular importance in relation to feminine development, remembering always that the gods, who were once projected outward and seen as external realities, are now to be found in the living web of the psyche. The more agriculture becomes mechanized, the more it is seen as a job for men, but the vast amount of cultivation has always been done by women. Men came onto the scene with the transformative plow, which simulates the sexual act with the "female" earth and thus gave rise to a whole new set of myths based on the divine marriage. But cultivation first developed out of gathering, as women's work, and women were then in the vanguard of human progress. The awe-inspiring process by which the seed is buried and appears to die, only to produce, in due season, abundant new growth and new grains, all this attended by rituals of soil preparation, watering, weeding and watching, and in accordance with rhythms that required intimate knowledge, all this was in the hands of woman, who became mistress of the fields and of abundance, and priestess of the mysteries of the life cycle.[75]

In other words, the feminine psyche developed with the discovery of agriculture, including also the processing and cooking of the produce. To give one example of the psychological import of this work, a number of fairy stories describe a woman's task of separating out different kinds of grains or lentils, or the good seed from the bad; metaphorically, this is the sorting out of things at the seed stage so that they don't cause mix-ups later.[76] This process of delicate and painstaking discrimination is characteristic of the development of feminine consciousness.

What are we to make of the Rice Krispie doll? Claire told me it was shaped like an undefined woman. In rice growing countries, a rice doll is sometimes made at the end of the harvest for the soul of

---

[75] See Mircea Eliade, *A History of Religious Ideas,* vol. 1, pp. 40f.
[76] Marie-Louise von Franz, *The Feminine in Fairy Tales,* pp. 156ff.

the Rice Goddess to inhabit until the new crop is sown or harvested. In Britain, the "corn dolly" plays a similar role. Traditionally, grains used in such an artifact are later sown, or fed to stock, as they are believed to increase fertility, so a bite of the doll could be expected to bring fruitfulness into the life of the eater. The doll is also tied up with the secret of where life goes when it is invisible. It is a visible carrier of that mysterious life which dries up, is destroyed and consumed, buried and resurrected, the botanical and agricultural process conveying metaphorically the equally mysterious process of psychic renewal. The relevant myth that still seems full of vitality in the Western psyche is that of Demeter and her daughter Persephone, who while picking flowers is seized by Hades and taken down by him to become queen of the Underworld.

Why the dream cereal is rice remains somewhat obscure. It did not particularly feature in Claire's life or upbringing, except as Rice Krispies; she described it simply as the main foodstuff of a large percentage of the world's population. Perhaps it is important that it comes from farther away than the grains of her own culture, and therefore relates to a process which is a little farther from consciousness. The childhood connotations and the connection with her grandmother are obviously important, linking her personal experience of mothering with the mythical figure. It is also significant that some time earlier Claire had had a dream in which she came to see me and found some other women present, and a buffet meal of which one of the main ingredients was white rice. This clearly prefigures the dream of the gathering of women around the Rice Krispie woman and places the rice in the context of the analysis.

At the time of the first dream Claire had said that she found plain white rice rather unappetizing, and in a dream soon after it she was throwing away left-over white rice after a dinner party; there was obviously more of it than she could stomach. A propos of Rice Krispie cakes she said they were more interesting than plain rice. A subtle but important shift had happened, for now she wanted more; perhaps I had presented something in a more palatable way.

One of the themes of the dream is that of being fed by the Good

Mother, with whom Claire had had so little contact. She was finding something nourishing in the analytic work; she was able to assimilate more readily. But here it is not the Fruit Mother, who connects us with that glorious state of oneness and the primal, natural surge of life; it is the Grain Mother, who teaches of engagement with the soil out of which new life can come. The themes of coming down to earth and of eating the piece of the Rice Krispie doll both relate to that process of becoming more solid which the alchemists called *coagulatio*.[77]

There are times when we need to rise up and contemplate things from above *(sublimatio)*, but at this stage in Claire's process the dream has to do with the value of being grounded. It is time for more of a "hands-on" approach. That she was ready for this was confirmed by her next dream, in which she stood barefoot on the ground, playfully tracing lines with a rake on a pile of black, moist earth. She had never brought such an earthy dream before.

To include the whole of Claire's dream would involve too many excursions, but immediately after the contact with the Rice Krispie woman the dreamer is making her way home and fears she is being followed by a man. Here there is just a hint of the Demeter/Persephone myth and the looming presence of Hades. That Hades might be in the vicinity would refer to the possibility of descent. Below the world of concrete reality and of the grain field lies the world of shadowy, insubstantial forms that we are dimly aware of, the world of the unconscious. To be in touch with the queen of the Underworld would mean a new valuing of this strange but rich domain. (Hades is also Pluto, "wealth.")

Moreover, it is the daughter's descent that enables her to separate from mother. Inevitably, when a woman has a negative image of her mother, there is a distressing unconscious similarity that needs to be made conscious if it is not to be destructive. This is one aspect of the work of separating. Another is the ability to differentiate the

---

[77] For an excellent account of this process, with specific mention of food imagery, see Edward F. Edinger, *Anatomy of the Psyche,* chap. 4.

maternal from the joyously, playfully girlish, as different manifestations of feminine nature. In this drama Hades would be a downward-directed counterpart to the pilot that takes the dreamer up.

Vegetarianism

Living on a purely vegetable diet has only been a possibility since the development of agriculture and with a distancing from our "animal nature," which simply takes what it can unreflectingly. But is vegetarianism a nostalgic harking back to a mythical age of innocence or a step forward into a new kind of consciousness?

We have seen that discomfort at killing to eat is as old as humanity, but that this is crucially tied in with the development of ritual and social cohesion. "I would say," writes Rafael López-Pedraza, "that killing animals with weapons, religious ritual, and mythological thinking together compose a basic and conflictive complex in humankind."[78] Once a reliable vegetable diet becomes available, however, separating slaughter from nutritive requirements, there arises the new possibility of compassion for animal suffering being experienced in a new way, unmixed with fear that the slaughtered beast might take revenge. Among the Greeks and Romans there were those who experienced such compassion acutely:

> He who can slit his calf's throat, hear its cries
> Unmoved, who has the heart to kill his kid
> That screams like a small child, or eat the bird
> His hand has reared and fed! How far does this
> Fall short of murder?[79]

As these lines imply, a link tends to be felt between violence toward animals and violence toward humans, so that meat eating is often connected with aggression generally, and with warlike behavior. It has been noted above that hunting and warfare are closely linked. Vegetarianism by contrast is frequently supposed to induce a peaceful nature.

---

[78] *Hermes and His Children*, p. 51.

[79] Ovid, *The Doctrines of Pythagoras*, quoted in Colin Spencer, *The Heretic's Feast: A History of Vegetarianism*, p. 98.

Living without meat, moreover, has always tended to suggest a further distancing from the animal. No article of food has attracted more prohibitions and cautions imposed by the demands of good manners than meat. Picking up in the hand a greasy piece of flesh and bone and tearing at it with the teeth has long had a dubious reputation as "animal behavior," and where once the conspicuous carving of a whole animal on or in sight of the table was looked upon with pleasure, this process has in Western culture tended to retreat behind the scenes, while in China and Japan such barbarisms were confined to the kitchen much earlier, along with the potentially threatening knife, in favor of delicate eating with chopsticks.[80]

Distancing ourselves from our animal nature tends to imply an approach toward the spiritual, and from the time of Pythagoras this has always been an important connotation of vegetarianism. The Neo-Platonist Porphyry argued that a meat diet was unsuitable for the philosopher; perhaps the philosophical ideal would be not to have to eat at all, an achievement claimed by certain saints. To refrain from eating meat has regularly been associated with spiritual commitment, along with that other carnal act, sex, and has also implied a degree of asceticism. From this point of view meat feeds the baser, more earth-bound aspects of mankind. Within Christianity, abstention from meat on prescribed days has always been intended as self-denial or penance, rather than concern for animal welfare.

The question is, though, how far away from animal behavior can we get, since we are undeniably animals and not disembodied spirits? López-Pedraza observes of vegetarians that they have

> a fantasy of purity and cleanliness, a rigidity, a feeling of superiority, a guilt-making projection upon meat-eaters, and a lack of consciousness of any cruelty and destructiveness in themselves.[81]

The viciousness with which supporters of vegetarianism and animal welfare sometimes express themselves demonstrates the ag-

---

[80] This evolution of table manners is recorded in fascinating detail by Elias in his classic book *The Civilising Process.*
[81] *Hermes,* pp. 22f.

gressive shadow. Cruelty and destructiveness belong to us, and we had better recognize that if we are to avoid endless bitter entanglements through shadow-projection. If we follow the morality of vegetarianism to the ultimate conclusion we must face the fact that dairy produce involves the premature and distressing separation of young from mother, and the slaughter of young males. Nor are foods the only animal products in common use. The development of humanity is inseparable from the use and abuse of other species on a massive scale, through their labor and through the uses of their carcasses, so we are all profoundly implicated in this business, and indebted to it, whether we like it or not. As a race we are a very long way from dispensing with all these dependencies. Vegetarians must look into their own inconsistencies and hypocrisies if they are not to fall into fantasies of superiority.

In Buddhist Tibet, where vegetables have been scarce and meat eating a virtual necessity, those who had taken vows of nonkilling were permitted to eat meat as long they did not kill it themselves. In consequence the butchers on whom they depended were usually Muslims, onto whom the guilt could be shuffled in the same way that Jews in Christendom were made to carry the guilt of usury.

Furthermore, at this point most of us assume that plants are not sentient. We have left behind the old animistic beliefs that plants had souls, which meant that gathering and agriculture were attended by guilt feelings similar to those surrounding animal slaughter, and required propitiation. Recently, however, it has been suggested that plants respond to the shock of assault much as animals do, as if silently screaming.[82]

How we relate to the slaughter of animals is a matter of conscience, but we would do well to remember the inextricability of life and death, survival and destruction, and that in fleeing from animal suffering we are also fleeing from our own. Because of the inseparability of the development of culture from meat eating, vegetarianism has always attracted disapproval from the meat eating

---

[82] See, for instance, John Whitman, *The Psychic Power of Plants,* pp. 41ff.

establishment. In the context of classical Greece, to refuse to eat meat was

> not only to behave in a manner different from one's fellows, it [was] to decide not to carry out the most important act in civil religion [i.e., that of sacrifice], for the two were inseparable, legitimate meat deriving solely from beasts ritually slaughtered in the presence of gods and men.[83]

The Pythagoreans and Orphics, by opting out of this practice were making a social and religious statement that isolated them. In Rome, Seneca and Ovid, two proponents of a meat-free diet, were persecuted for their unconventionality.[84] Vegetarians later became suspect in the eyes of the Christian church as likely supporters of heresies (Manicheans or Cathars).

Vegetarianism can still arouse strong feelings in our meat eating culture, even in Britain where it is so common that a recent report suggests that forty per cent of schoolchildren are vegetarians. The meat and dairy industries, in defending their commercial interests, call upon millennia of cultural resistance to abstention from meat. In 1992 an English newspaper reported that the Minister of Agriculture "has described vegetarian diets as 'faddist and *unnatural* and the [Meat and Livestock Commission] has said the Vegetarian Society is a *danger to democracy.'* "[85] Consequent to recent protests against the veal trade, in certain milieus to be a vegan is seen as tantamount to being a terrorist.

To understand the recent surge of vegetarianism, we should note the important ecological pressures and the relative wastefulness of stock raising compared to meeting our nutritional needs directly from the produce of the fields, and also put it in the context of current meat-eating practice. In the past, in most settled communities all over the world, meat has been a relative rarity, a luxury item.

---

[83] Detienne, "Culinary Practices and the Spirit of Sacrifice," in Detienne and Vernant, *The Cuisine of Sacrifice Among the Greeks*, p. 6.

[84] See Spencer, *The Heretic's Feast*, p. 96.

[85] "School Leaflet Against Meat Under Attack" (italics added), in *The Independent*, London, 14 July 1992.

The decision to slaughter one of the stock was not taken lightly, and hunting expeditions brought in only occasional prized beasts, every bit of which would find a use. The reality of the relationship between food and death was part of everyone's experience, together with the mixed feelings of pleasure and guilt. The ready availability of prepackaged supermarket meat and the distance of the average city dweller from the live animal and the slaughtering process has meant that the meat-eater can enjoy considerable protection from feelings of guilt concerning the animal's death. Meanwhile, split off from collective consciousness, the quality of life of the typical food animal has diminished, often grotesquely, and the circumstances surrounding its death have arguably become far more terrible.

Though some of its members may simplistically imagine that to refrain from meat is to refrain from being destructive, the vegetarian movement has brought back into general awareness the conflict surrounding the consumption of meat. Re-relating to the suffering animal is no doubt also an attempt to reconnect with and respect our own ill-treated instinctual nature.

A la Carte

The nineteenth-century French gastronome Brillat-Savarin declared, "Dis-moi ce que tu manges, je te dirai ce que tu es."[86] We might compare this with the epigraph to this chapter, the advice from the *I Ching* to pay heed to the providing of nourishment, and to what a man seeks to fill his own mouth with, further explained by Richard Wilhelm: "If we wish to know what anyone is like, we have only to observe on whom he bestows care and what sides of his own nature he cultivates and nourishes."[87]

Somewhere scientific dietetics (subject to constant revision) merges with collective and individual projections onto foodstuffs: fish is good for the brain, beef makes you manly or aggressive, oysters are an aphrodisiac, "no sugar, thanks, I'm sweet enough as I

---

[86] "Tell me what you eat and I'll tell you who you are." *Physiologie du Goût*, p. 5.

[87] *The I Ching or Book of Changes*, pp. 107f.

am." What we eat can be associated with which gods we serve. Who are we nurturing when we nurture "ourselves"? A woman with an ulcer took to eating baby food. It was the baby that really wanted feeding. Following the classification developed by anthropologist Mary Douglas, Gerald and Valerie Mars explore what eating habits tell us about the eaters: individualists demonstrate their eclecticism, hierarchists their attachment to tradition, egalitarians reject the wicked outside with, for example, ostentatious veganism, fatalists eat whatever comes to their attention.[88]

Whether we are feeding our individualism or our traditional values, our ethical judgments or our nonchalance, what we take in through our mouths tells us something about where we direct our energy. After his long practice of asceticism failed to achieve the desired result, the Buddha turned from feeding the spirit and starving the body—he accepted some milk-rice from a woman. In so doing he was not only being fed by but also feeding the earth mother, not living on spirit alone. Then he attained enlightenment, for in abandoning his one-sided striving he had discovered the middle way; he was honoring both heaven and earth, spirit and body.

---

[88] See Mars and Mars, "Two Contrasting Dining Styles."

3
Eating Together

> In hell people find themselves in front of wonderful food, but with such long spoons that they don't reach the mouth. In heaven they use the long spoons to feed each other.—Jewish saying.

Eating is traditionally largely something we do with others. This is a distinctly human trait, for while other species feed their young, the adults generally fend for themselves individually. The African wild dog is like us an exception, sharing a kill amicably, but chimpanzees after a successful hunt are like most hunters: they hustle to get some of the kill, or wait in the hope of leftovers. Sharing food is an act of social commitment which involves self-restraint, and seems likely to have developed in the context of eating large animals and using tools. "Fruitarians have no need to develop these chivalrous instincts."[89] Among hunter-gatherers a kill is shared.

Sharing food is a fundamental bonding ritual in which we affirm our common identity as members of a family or group. In the Passover *seder,* for example, a Jewish family affirms continuity of tradition despite severe dislocations, and through the consumption of unleavened bread and bitter herbs expresses identity with the ancestors, bringing the symbolism of their significant experiences into connection with the present.

Michel Tournier's book *Le Médianoche Amoureux* culminates in a story called "The Two Banquets," in which the caliph of Isfahan chooses between two applicants for the role of principle cook at his palace. They each prepare a banquet. The first is exquisite, but the second exactly replicates the first. The caliph appoints the second cook as "priest of the kitchen," for he has understood the sacred nature of repetition.

This tale is told within the framework of an outer story concern-

---

[89] Morgan, *Descent of Woman,* p. 24.

ing a couple whose marriage has become silent and stale. They give a party for all their friends, intending to conclude it by announcing their forthcoming divorce. Throughout the night the guests tell stories. Stories from real life, with their bitter tang, confirm the couple in their decision, but later stories of the imagination mysteriously draw them closer together, and the announcement of their separation fails to materialize. The clincher is "The Two Banquets." The association between meals, story-telling, ritual and eros is revealed, and the husband and wife rediscover the meaning inherent in everyday routine. In real life, recipes, like stories, are handed on to become the substance of tradition, bringing us together in appreciation and companionship.

Festivals have often involved the whole community assembling to eat a common meal. In Greece, for example, certain local festivals still involve food being served in the church, bringing the whole village together in communal kinship. The Christian Eucharist, like other sacramental meals, expresses the solidarity of the initiates. In societies where men and women eat apart the meal serves the cohesion of the male or female group. In India, where the Hindu rules of conduct forbade eating outside one's caste, the Sikhs introduced communal eating places where these divisions were no longer maintained. A com*pan*ion is someone with whom we eat bread, our cultural staple, and in a similar vein the Japanese talk of "eating rice out of the same pot." The dipping of Jesus' hand into the dish along with Judas's emphasizes the bond between them which is to be betrayed.

Continuity with the ancestral past and the psychic presence of the recently departed is acknowledged in the practice of inviting the dead once more to eat with the living. The ancient Greeks served *nekrodeipna* to the recently departed, and such practices are still widespread, a special day often being laid aside for communion with the dead. In Egypt, for example, families picnic by the graves of their relatives, and in many parts of the world special "soul cakes" are baked. Best known perhaps is the Mexican Day of the Dead, a colorful festival involving artifacts, costumes and flowers as well as food offerings. A special kind of bread and painstakingly prepared cooked dishes and beverages are laid out on the decorated, tiered offering table. When the souls have invisibly extracted the essence of the food it is shared among the living. This bonding with the dead reinforces a sense of continuity with the past, and, by providing a framework within which the dead can be remembered and made placated, also provides some protection for the living from the potentially dangerous effects connected with them being split off in the unconscious.

While bonding the eaters, food also distinguishes them from others. Our traditional dishes emphasize our group identity, but so do those foods we culturally deny ourselves—they are the food of alien people, unclean, repulsive, bizarre or ridiculous. Few cultural characteristics make a stronger impression on the traveler than food customs, and denigrating references to the traditional diet of others serves our xenophobia. "I've nothing against them, it's the smell of their food." We nickname cultural groups according to what they eat. The British call the French "frogs" and the Germans "krauts," while the French refer to the British as *les rosbifs.* The word "Eskimo" is a corruption of a North American Indian word meaning "eater of raw flesh," and the Mennonites who have migrated from Mexico to Ontario are derided as "taco-eaters."

> A small number of white men lived in Fort Yukon. These men had been long in the country. They called themselves Sour-doughs. For other men, new in the land, they felt nothing but disdain. The men who came ashore from the steamers were newcomers. They were known as *chechaquos,* and they always wilted at the application of this name. They made their bread with baking-powder. This was the invidious distinction between them and the Sour-doughs, who, forsooth, made their bread from sour-dough because they had no baking-powder.[90]

What is considered proper food for humans is variable. The parsnip is an honored vegetable in Britain, but scorned as "animal food" by the Swiss, while in the West generally that important sta-

---

[90] Jack London, *White Fang,* p. 242.

ple millet is bird seed, fit only for budgies. To eat the food of another culture is a step toward assimilation; advertising for an American fast-food chain in Japan suggested that it would make Japanese consumers blond and tall, clearly aiming to exploit certain aspirations by an appeal to a primitive layer of the psyche. The rice-based diet of the Indians, warned Brillat-Savarin, made them soft and cowardly and a pushover for conquerors.[91] It has also often been claimed that peasant food would coarsen the aristocrat and aristocratic food make the peasant ill, that one must eat according to one's station. Massimo Montanari retells a story from a fourteenth-century novella by Sabadino degli Arienti in which a peasant steals peaches from his master's garden. He is punished and told, "In future leave my fruit alone and eat your own foods, which are turnips, garlic, leeks, onions and shallots with sorghum bread."[92]

Since our stomachs demand food at frequent intervals, the opportunity to participate in the culinary rituals of our particular culture presents itself, if we are lucky, several times a day, at culturally determined times, so that this affirmation of our group membership becomes routine. We have seen how, according to Gerald and Valerie Mars, the individualists, traditionalists, egalitarians and fatalists consciously or unconsciously declare their group affiliations.

Universally, a marriage, as the union not only of bride and groom but also of two families, involves the coming together of both sides to share a meal in demonstration of their new kinship. Sitting down to eat together means putting aside differences, hence taboos on raising controversial issues at dinner parties. The dinner table can be a healing place where opponents discover each others' common humanity. It is a place where relationship is fed and warm personal exchanges take place. A rabbi once said that when he died he wanted to be buried in his dining-room table, as he had spent the happiest moments of his life there.

Even the business lunch seeks to capitalize on this harmonizing

---

[91] *Physiologie du Goût*, p. 57.
[92] *The Culture of Food*, p. 86.

effect to create an atmosphere in which agreement can be reached. A small miracle happened in 1993 when Prime Minister Rabin of Israel and Yasha Arafat, leader of the Palestinian Liberation Organization, were invited to Norway, away from the uncompromising political atmosphere of their homelands. They spent time eating and walking together in pleasant surroundings, arriving at an agreement to take back to their peoples.

Just who is invited to the table is a thorny question. We prefer to ask only those we feel comfortable with, but those excluded may take offense and cause trouble. At the wedding of Peleus and Thetis, honored by the presence of the twelve Olympians, Eris (Strife) was understandably left out. She gate-crashed the party anyway and stirred up competitiveness between Hera, Athene and Aphrodite, which led to the Trojan war. At the birth feast of the princess in "Sleeping Beauty," only twelve wise women were summoned. The thirteenth arrived uninvited and delivered her curse. The awkward element we ban from consciousness has a way of popping up at an inconvenient moment. Better to give it a seat at the party where we can keep an eye on it. The mother who had forbidden her son to mention a delicate matter at table breathed a sigh of relief when he went off to play, thinking she had banned the demon; turning to her guest she asked, "Will you have custard with your wart?"

On the other hand we may make the uninvited guest welcome. A woman dreamed:

> I'm in a room with a big table with a lot of people sitting round it. I can't remember in detail who's there, but it's the usual crowd of friends. Next to me there's an empty chair.

Who knows who the stranger at the door might be? Jews keep a chair for Elijah at the *seder*. In Greece before the last war people always kept a place for Jesus or the stranger. This willingness to entertain the new cannot coexist with defensive stuckness.

The existence of rules governing hospitality is universal. The words "host" and "guest" have essentially the same root, as can be seen in the French *hôte*, which has both meanings; the roles are in-

terchangeable, either way a bond is established, attended by obligations. *Hostis,* the Latin word for guest, corresponding to the Gothic
gasts and Old Slavonic *gosti,* originally meant a stranger who stood
in a compensatory or reciprocal relationship, someone who could
return the compliment.[93] The ideas of exchange and equality were
inherent in the term.

The Greeks saw host and guest as adherents to a kind of pact
involving an exchange of gifts; this *xenia* was under the protection
of Zeus Xenios and was also binding on descendants. Paris's crime
was that he violated the sacred contract by seducing his host's wife.
The Iranian word for guest, *meh-man,* is related to the Latin *munus,*
a public office involving an obligation to finance entertainments for
the people, at root "a gift carrying the obligation of exchange." A
community is thus "a group of persons united by this bond of
reciprocity," and a communion is a rite that cements it.[94]

The Arabs say that anyone you have taken salt with is always a
friend; in English we speak of people we have broken bread with.
The guest must also receive appreciatively, for the host is offering
friendship; to refuse that is to create enmity. An acquaintance who
was overwhelmed by the number of courses at a Moroccan banquet
and tried to excuse himself on grounds of a weak stomach was told
firmly, "The food of friends is medicine." People on restrictive diets can cause discomfort at table as they are not fully participating.
It takes an effort of consciousness to detach the principles of sharing and generosity from the concrete substance of food, to appreci-
ate that equivalent exchange can take place in a more subtle way;
and that to force food on a person who does not want it or might be
harmed by it is mean spirited.

Choosing to eat with someone is everywhere regarded as a serious matter, not to be taken lightly. "He needs a long spoon who
sups with the Devil." A woman dreamed that she was in a big, ele-
gant house belonging to unknown, powerful people whom she was

---

[93] See Emile Benveniste, *Indo-European Language and Society,* pp. 71ff.
[94] Ibid.

invited to join for a meal. She felt flattered. When she eventually came to the dining room it was full of zombie-like figures dressed as monks who had to take turns in eating, and she was expected to join them. The atmosphere was unpleasant, and the dreamer feared becoming like the uniform eaters, so she refrained. The seductive invitation to join the powerful unconscious elements, so seemingly attractive, to identify with them by sharing their food, would lead the dreamer to dreary conformity and meanness of nourishment, associated perhaps with a phony spirituality. Fortunately she recognizes the danger and refuses to participate.

Jeannette, a single woman in her early forties, had this dream:

> I am sitting at table with my mother and grandmother. My mother has prepared a pineapple by removing the skin. Each of us eats a quarter of the fruit. The last slice has to be kept for an unknown woman who will use it as a container in some sort of rite.

Jeannette had come into therapy with chronic depression, trying to understand why she was unable to find either a partner to settle down with or the inner resources to feel fulfilled on her own. She had been brought up by her maternal grandmother and her depressed mother, and despised the latter for her fearful and negative attitude toward life. The mother had never recovered from the early breakdown of her marriage and had thereafter cut herself off from the world as far as possible. She lived in isolation with her own widowed mother.

The three women of the dream evoke the triple form of the goddess as maid, mother and crone, as well as the chain that links the female line. Jeannette's only personal association to the pineapple was its use as a decorative motif on a building she had often walked past with a married man she had loved, but who had ultimately returned to his wife. Classically the pineapple is associated with Cybele, the great mother goddess of Asia Minor. It is made up of numerous small fruits grown into one and hence is a representation of the many in one, like the pomegranate, another fruit associated with feminine deities.

Jeannette remarked that her mother in fact would never have

served a fresh pineapple as she did in the dream; she would have opened a can. The dream points back from the twentieth-century personal mother to an archetypal figure. In talking about this dream, and about what it might mean to be sharing food with her mother, Jeannette realized with a shock how much she, like her mother, had withdrawn from life, making herself unavailable and denying herself meaningful activity. Eating her mother's food meant staying in a state of unconscious identification, not fully born into her individuality, condemned to share the lonely fate of mother and grandmother. The dream points the way out of this situation, suggesting that energy be diverted to the unknown woman.

A meal can be an opportunity to interact freely or, on the other hand, to manifest rank, as we have seen in the apportioning of meat. The select few may eat separately in the executive dining room or at the high table. Seating plans make clear who is privileged to be close to the head of the table, above the salt, and the most important people enter the room first, are served first, and must start before others. In the English upper-class dining room, for example, it is not unknown for squabbles to break out over such questions as whether the cousin of a baron should take precedence over the daughter of a baronet. The issue of hierarchy was neatly tackled by the legendary King Arthur with his egalitarian round table. Obligations follow the receipt of favored invitations from one's superiors, for the law of reciprocity still maintains that there's no free lunch. "When thou sittest to eat with a ruler, consider diligently what is before thee. . . . Be not desirous of his dainties: for they are deceitful meat." (Prov. 23:1, 3)

The table is traditionally a major focus in the socialization of children, where they must learn self-restraint and deference and the rules of the clan, and the table of our childhood is often the location of concentrated memories of family. Bad experiences there can lead to social phobia at communal meals or restaurants. A successful professional man found himself unable to eat with clients, or at family celebrations, without being seized by stomach pains or nausea. Such occasions constellated the oppressive father whose rules of conduct were absolute and whose punishment for transgressions was devastating.

A woman who had at last succeeded in finding her own identity, separating from parental expectations and freeing herself from the effects of a stifling family background, had a dream in which she returned to her childhood home and repainted it, after which she was able to leave it and look back with sadness at her parents still inside. She painted the whole house white, and put in cream or stone-colored carpets, but she hesitated in the dining room, which had a red carpet (as had been the case in reality). This was the room in which the whole family used to gather, including grandparents, and where the mother was in her element, rejoicing in her family and receiving praise for her cooking. The warm red glow of family togetherness was the most difficult regressive pull to overcome, the dining room the most resistant to transformation.

The table is an evocative image. The following comes from a dream located in the house the dreamer shared with her partner:

> I am struck by the bad state of repair of a piece of furniture provided by my parents, it's a kind of weird, black table . . . battered, chipped, cheap. I think it will have to go.

Her first association to "table" was that "it brings people together." This inherited table did not seem likely to make a very good job of it, an old structure that had had its day.

Meals eaten together and traditional, ritual menus embody social stability. In societies today where the larger family group has been broken up and even the "nuclear" family is frequently incomplete, where mothers have little time for food preparation, the regular family meal is often replaced by fast food. For many people growing up now the table will have lost its traditional significance. The lack of social cohesion is mirrored in irregular eating patterns, sandwiches gulped down on commuter trains, breakfast taken standing at a kitchen counter, foods that come in prepackaged portions, meals-on-wheels eaten in isolation. When people live alone, as so many do now, they often neglect to cook at all. When food is not prepared for sharing we lose an important ritual way of expressing our social identity and affection for others.

On the other hand, we now have greater flexibility, liberation from the tyranny of set mealtimes and an alimentary eclecticism matched by the possibility of relatively free social exchange. To what group we declare our membership through the kinship of the table and the recipes we offer is now more a question of choice.

4
Assimilation

Some books are to be tasted, others are to be swallowed, and some few to be chewed and digested.—Francis Bacon.

Perhaps the most aggressive way you can relate to what is not you, completely establish your will over it, is to eat it. In the process its integrity is destroyed; it is dismembered mechanically and broken down chemically into smaller and smaller molecules by the action of enzymes from the salivary glands, stomach, pancreas and intestines. You assimilate it; that is to say, it is converted into your body, digested. The word digest itself comes from Latin *digerere,* meaning to take apart. "It" ceases to exist. The serial murderer Jeffrey Dahmer said he ate his victims in order to satisfy his desire to have total control over them.

What you eat has its effect, helpful or harmful. In the Hippocratic Corpus of ancient Greek medical writings it is remarked that

> each one of the substances of a man's diet acts upon his body and changes it in some way and upon these changes his whole life depends whether he be in health, in sickness, or convalescent.[95]

Current medical theory itself breaks down what we eat into fats, carbohydrates, proteins, vitamins and minerals, and aims to define the effect each component has, in what quantity and in what combinations. Medicine has always considered diet important in maintaining health and treating illness, though the highly sophisticated Indian ayurvedic system is singular in its emphasis on dietary medicine. It classifies all edible items in various ways, and prescribes them to counteract particular imbalances in the body. Dream food serves this function at the psychic level, but who prescribes it?

---

[95] *Hippocratic Writings,* p. 78.

The psyche has its own way of seeing the influence on us of what we eat. This is recognizable from our dreams and stories, and from our projections onto food. Aphrodisiacs, for example, as carriers of our erotic wishes, are often thought to be so because they resemble male or female genitalia. The moist and hidden oyster is a current instance of the latter, while according to Margaret Visser, in the Nile Valley the lettuce is still popularly believed to promote male fertility, having once been associated with the Egyptian fertility god Min. The local variety of lettuce was phallically pointed, and moreover the lettuce produces a milky fluid analogous to semen.[96] The signature of its therapeutic quality is visible in the plant. Eat lettuce and you will acquire its qualities of erection and production. The Doctrine of Correspondences may not be true empirically, but it is certainly true at the level of imagination.

The fantasy that by eating we acquire the characteristics of our food is widespread. James George Frazer writes:

> Some of the Brazilian Indians would eat no beast, bird or fish, that ran, flew, or swam slowly, lest partaking of its flesh they should lose their agility and be unable to escape from their enemies. The Caribs . . . . refused to partake of tortoises from a fear that if they did so they would become heavy and stupid like the animal.[97]

In a dream during the course of psychotherapy a fight occurred between snakes and cats. It appeared that the snakes had won and devoured the cats, for then the snakes, which had now become furry, approached the dreamer and rubbed themselves against her like cats, and despite some fear she stooped to pick them up. The snakes ate the cats and became cat-like, as if warm-blooded, domestic. The more archaic, more deeply unconscious component had won out temporarily, but this led to a counter-movement bringing the contents closer to consciousness so that they could be embraced. In a somewhat similar fashion, in Greek mythology Zeus first marries Metis and later, fearing the fulfillment of predictions concern-

---

[96] See *Much Depends on Dinner,* pp. 194f.
[97] *The Golden Bough: A Study in Magic and Religion,* pp. 649, 651.

ing their future child, eats her. His conquest of her is in a sense complete, but she continues a quasi-existence within him and advises him from his belly. He acquires her wisdom and also her ability to give birth.

It seems then that assimilation as understood by the psyche is a two-way process; that is to say, the eater is also assimilated to the eaten. The nearest nature comes to this is illustrated by the flatworm *Microstomum caudatum,* which feeds on the freshwater polyp *Hydra* and absorbs the stinging cells of the *Hydra* whole, separating them from the rest of the body which passes through the flatworm's digestive process. "They are then deposited on the body surface of the flatworm, where they serve as a kind of pirated defence mechanism."[98]

Such literal acquisition of the physical characteristics of the eaten is a rarity in the world of matter, but metaphorically it conveys a psychological truth. When we take something in we tend to take on some of its qualities, or are influenced by it.

The body I feed is what I point to, to indicate "I" (ego). This is the shape of me; the skin is my boundary, the orifices points of entry or exit between me and others. This is true of the imaginal as well as of the physical body. Taking in, incorporating, introjecting something from the outside has the purpose of integrating it into this "me." In the course of the psychological digestive process I make it my own; it comes to form part of my identity. Nothing of course is ever completely assimilated, physiologically or psychologically. Some of it will be discarded. Nor, despite the fact that the ego is the center of consciousness, is the process an entirely conscious one. A large part of the assimilation takes place out of sight in that hidden inner laboratory, the unconscious.

It might be asked at what point in this peristaltic and enzymatic activity the something other that I ingest becomes me, but at that level one can no longer think in terms of self and other, only of chemical or psychic processes.

---

[98] *The Oxford Companion to Animal Behaviour,* p. 210.

In assimilating experiences with all their emotional content, factual information and ideas, we may meet difficulties which can be expressed imaginally in digestive terms, or even through physical alimentary problems. We might take an example from Jung's autobiography, in which he mentions an infectious enteritis that affected him in North Africa, and which he saw as psychosomatic. It can be understood as a reflection of his struggle to assimilate the onslaught of new impressions.[99]

In the process of assimilation, "all haste is of the devil," as the alchemists said. Good digestion requires a state of relative tranquillity. In anxiety states, when the "flight-or-fight" mechanisms are stimulated, blood flows to the muscles of the back, arms and legs, while digestive processes are suppressed, hence the familiar association between anxiety and digestive problems (appetite loss, dry mouth, *globus hystericus,* butterflies and knots in the stomach, diarrhea, loss of bowel control, etc.). It has been shown that the taking in of information is inhibited during states of arousal as measured by the heart rate.[100] As the effect dies away we begin to be able to digest the experience, integrate it into our psychic fabric, and the fire of emotion can produce the light of consciousness. The illness or depression that strikes after a period of stress forces us to slow down and give ourselves time to absorb what has happened.

Let us look more closely at the assimilative process of learning. We take in facts and ideas which may be more or less digestible. We analyze them consciously, compare the new intake with previously absorbed or evolved material, but for much of this process we have to rely on the unconscious to make connections. Eventually we may be in a position to apply the new knowledge, but it will now be our version of it. There will be bits of it we have consciously rejected, and aspects that somehow haven't fitted into our preexisting body of understanding, but if we have not "made it our

---

[99] *Memories, Dreams, Reflections,* p. 270.

[100] Lacey et al., "The Visceral Level: Situational Determinants and Behavioural Correlates of Autonomic Response Patterns." I am indebted to Michael Chance, who refers to the paper in an unpublished manuscript, 1993.

own" we will not be able to put it to use, only to regurgitate it. Similarly, if we read something in "digest" form we forfeit the possibility of digesting it for ourselves.

My restaurant dream, referred to earlier,[101] can be seen as having to do with this digesting of theory. It ran as follows:

> I go back to a restaurant where I have left volume eight of Jung's Collected Works on the table. At a nearby table are some students who invite me to join them. I sit down next to a young woman wearing ice-blue, pointed, high-heeled satin shoes, of the kind worn with evening dress. The young man opposite her suggests they go to a fashionable place where chess is played. She is eager to join in. I say, "I prefer to observe ."

A restaurant is a place of assimilation, also a public place, but not indiscriminately collective as a street or market would be. It holds a limited number of diners, may be selective about whom it admits, and is only open to those who can afford its prices. The dream restaurant seemed to be a small and fairly expensive one; it was reminiscent of a certain gourmet venue where I had been privileged to eat a number of times while at university, and where I had enjoyed some searching discussions. One goes to such a restaurant to choose from a particular menu, and Jung was apparently on the dream menu.

At the time of the dream I was reading Jung's essay, "Synchronicity: An Acausal Connecting Principle," which I had first read as an undergraduate many years earlier; now I was going back for it, this time apparently taking it home to read in a more personal space. The young people evoked the student life, and the girl with the cool standpoint of the ice-blue shoes, which would neither have been comfortable nor provided a very secure contact with the ground, was reminiscent of myself at that age. Following the suggestion of her male companion she was eager to be involved in playing an intellectual game (chess). This was also a question of fashionability, like her shoes, which were ready precariously to join

---

[101] Above, p. 25.

the dance. The allusion to intellectual game playing was a hint of the dangers of competitiveness. The dream states that now I have gained a position from which to observe, but it still goes on.

Theory can of course assimilate *us* while we think the reverse is happening. Again it is often the emotion a theory arouses in us which can hamper the psychic enzymes. Overzealous espousal of a body of ideas or beliefs without that inner work of discrimination and breaking down for absorption means feeding the dogma at the expense of our individual judgment, often in the guise of offering something valuable or liberating to others. As scientologists, evangelists, Marxists or existentialists we become clumsy slaves of a simplified system, sucked into a collective complex; we lose our integrity and our grip on reality, consumed by passion.

The Alimentary Process

The Mouth: The Way In

The gateway to the alimentary canal is the mouth, which, economically, along with the throat, also serves the function of voice production and speech formation. A large part of the sensory cortex is associated with this part of the body. It is a large and conspicuous orifice, and we are a little sensitive to the sight of it being opened wide to reveal the buccal cavity. This is permissible for singing, but generally unwelcome at feeding time, when it reminds us of our primitive needs and perhaps hints at the horrors of being devoured. It is not the only means by which we ingest the constituents needed to maintain the body—the nose and skin also serve—but it takes in the grosser, more obvious elements. Through the nose we take in air, but breath is spirit; what goes in through the maternal cave of the mouth is matter.

In its maternal symbolism the mouth can also be a kind of vagina, especially where the birth-giver is masculine. For example, images of that mysterious vegetative figure the Green Man often show him apparently producing foliage from his mouth, and it is the mouth of God that gives birth to the Word.

Our taste buds, located in the mucous membranes of tongue and palate, are a source of great pleasure and easily divert us into pleasing the mouth at the expense of the stomach. The first taste we learn to recognize as infants is sweetness. Sweets are an innocent pleasure of childhood, before we can imagine ourselves with false teeth, and both compulsive sweet eating and the consumption of sweetmeats in dreams may reflect desire for regression to this stage. As one of our deepest-rooted pleasure sensations, sweetness readily transfers itself metaphorically onto other objects of desire:

> Roses are red, violets are blue,
> Sugar is sweet and so are you.

Pop songs abound in endearments such as sweetheart, honey-bunch, sugar-pie and so on, as in a song made popular by The Band:

> Now there's one thing in the whole wide world
> I sure do love to see
> That's how that little sweet thing of mine
> Puts her donut in my tea.[102]

In Jewish tradition, honeyed apples are offered to sweeten the new year, while bitter herbs commemorate ancestral tribulations. "Sweeteners" are offered as inducements to deals, and the Chinese kitchen god Tsao Chun is offered sweetmeats on his annual trip to heaven so he will say only good things about the household. Usually the image of sweetness represents what we crave in life. At worst something may be *too* sweet, sickly, cloying, sentimental, but mostly we are happy if life is sweet rather than bitter or sour. To dream of eating something sweet can relate to assimilating pleasant truths, or, according to Edward Edinger, "that the time has come to bring certain conscious insights into concrete reality—to go for one's desires."[103]

But sweetness isn't everything. The salt of the earth and the spice of life are indispensable, and there's a place too for the sharp and the astringent, not to mention textures such as crisp or smooth

---

[102] "Up on Cripple Creek," by J.R. Robertson.
[103] *The Mysterium Lectures: A Journey through C.G. Jung's* Mysterium Coniunctionis, p. 289.

and creamy. Our personal taste is whatever gives us pleasure (and *de gustibus non est disputandum),* and where pleasure is frowned upon tasty foods are discouraged. Delicious can mean naughty, bad, self-indulgent. In Britain, "good, wholesome food" still has puritanical overtones of plain, unadulterated righteousness and the simple God-fearing life. A story by Karen Blixen, *Babette's Feast,* filmed in 1987 by Gabriel Axel, beautifully portrays the clash between virtue and voluptuousness when the heroine, a former chef from food-loving Paris, spends literally a small fortune on feasting her adoptive community of austere, pleasure-fearing Protestants.

The discriminating palate has more to do with refinements of pleasure than bodily well-being, more with Aphrodite than Hygeia. In ancient Egyptian, the hieroglyph for "nose" signified both "smell" and "taste" (which are of course closely linked physically) and also "enjoy," "take pleasure in." Good taste brings beauty and subtlety into our lives and smoothness into our relationships with others. Bad taste is shocking, abrasive, disgusting, though there may of course be a pleasure in deliberately cultivating it for effect.

A woman dreams she orders a bottle of cold beer. It is not just any beer, but a particular brand which is not only subtly flavored and attractive to the palate but also comes in a distinctive bottle, and this is part of the dreamer's anticipated pleasure. It is not the beverage downed in large quantities by bands of unruly males but a drink of some refinement which she plans to savor slowly. The dreamer is a woman of taste, and intends to feed her tastefulness as well as put a little spirit into herself. The barman, however (whom she associated to her bullying father), brings her a different kind of bottle, partly filled with a warmish, colorless liquid that smells unpleasantly of pure alcohol, saying, when she protests, that surely this is what she really wants. The implication is felt to be that she is only pretending social graces and just wants to get drunk.

At this point the dreamer becomes violently angry. The good taste has gone right out of the situation. Her desire for coolness and refinement is thwarted by this coarse, cynical inner man with his crude shortcut to loss of control, and he can only feed her rage. He is however the bearer of "pure" spirit and if befriended might be of inestimable value.

A large mouth is considered a sign of sensuality. Fleshy lips suggest both gluttony and lechery; smacked in anticipation of delicacies they also bespeak the voluptuous contact of kissing. Fashion models, whose physical desirability is used to enhance the designs they wear, are currently often required to have their lips injected with silicone to make them more luscious, like the famous "bee-stung" lips of the screen seductress Mae West. In iconographic convention holy figures are depicted with small mouths, appropriate for those who are above earthly concerns.

From soon after birth, nourishing substance regularly crosses the threshold of the mouth from outside to inside. Already in the womb the food orifice is preparing for this, one of the most basic tasks of infant life—the fetus sucks its thumb as it will soon in the outer world suck the breast, and not long after will inquisitively do the same with any proximate object ("suck it and see"). Much has been written on the development in the child of a sense of inside and outside, and Melanie Klein in particular relates this to the oral stage and its imagery. For her the inner world, though a rich territory, is essentially the product of introjection; as the reality without is incorporated it provides the substance for the images which compose inner reality. We develop interiority by feeding on the external. One may of course object that from the beginning our hidden inner reality is also busy creating the outer world but this is not an oral issue.

The metaphor of eating does refer to what we take in, one way or another, from the outer world, but it can also be that we are fed from inside, that our dream lips form a threshold over which the mysterious other can pass on the way to being incorporated into our sense of who we are, a strange fruit with an unfamiliar taste that lingers and haunts, a few drops of elixir with an elusive fragrance.

Saliva and Anticipation

Selecting choice morsels from the menu or catching the scents wafted from the kitchen tends to produce salivation, the excitation of the digestive process which Pavlov famously made use of in his dog experiment. Freshly-baked cakes may be mouth-watering, but slavering, slobbering, dribbling, drooling are for dogs, vampires, small children, the senile and the brain damaged. In imagination such activity reduces us to an uncontrollable instinct-driven self-lubricating machine, imperfectly designed.

To demonstrate a watering mouth is in bad taste. The product of the salivary glands serves us well, however. Saliva cleans the mouth. Its enzymes begin the breaking-down process, and its alkalinity counteracts the acidity of the stomach. It welcomes food into the reception chamber of the mouth and helps it on its way. A dry mouth can accompany anxiety, when the body is ill-prepared for eating. Spittle, though, also has a wide range of nonalimentary meanings. There is contemptuous spit expressing disgust, but also spit offered to welcome the rising sun. Spittle can carry the projection of powerful, essential soul-substance capable of averting the evil eye, and mythologically it may be seen as the life stuff out of which the world was created.

> Saliva is the water connotation of the spirit. Christ used spittle in making the ointment, mixing it with clay to heal the blind man. Spitting or blowing has a magic significance all over the world.[104]

Teeth and Tackling Things

The infant sucks, an activity we may be reduced to again in old age, but to eat solid food satisfactorily requires teeth, operated by powerful jaw muscles. We speak of an official or body or legislation as having "no teeth" when we want to suggest ineffectiveness.

Teeth, like hands, and presumably dating from before our ancestors had hands, are our basic tools and weapons. In piercing, tearing and cutting they are the models for knife and spear, and in grinding, for pestle, mortar and mill-wheel. When we get our teeth into something we go deeply into it; we attack our food, tackle a problem. The dream dentist, concerned with the condition of our psy-

---

[104] Jung, *Dream Analysis,* p. 221.

chological bite, is usually trying to assist us in coming to grips with life effectively. If our dream teeth are loose or falling out we are in danger of losing our hold on things.

Teeth are primary aggressive agents, masculine attributes of the maw of the Great Mother, of the *vagina dentata* or the "jaws of death." The size of a creature's jaws can impress us horribly, and certain animals are well designed in this respect to provoke a shudder, such as the wolf, the shark and the crocodile, whose mouth forms such a large and conspicuous part of its body,

> And welcomes little fishes in
> With gently smiling jaws.[105]

Gritting or grinding our teeth usually indicates anger or dogged, bone-crushing determination; habitually bitten-back anger can often be read in tight jaw muscles. Biting into something is the decisive moment of attack, when we take the object, or some of it, inside to be dismembered and absorbed. It is not a final decision, for if we have bitten off more than we can chew it can be spat out or thrown up, but these are afterthoughts or fail-safe devices in emergency. We bite in the expectation of devouring, and once bitten the object will not be the same thereafter.

Biting can of course be an act of pure aggression or defensiveness divorced from nutritive concerns. Male baboons use their canines for fighting, as do many other species. In snarling we show our teeth as a warning, and small children, not yet adept at manipulating sticks and stones have found their teeth an effective means of expressing anger or malice, often learning at the breast their power of inflicting pain. The relatively harmless and often pleasure-giving act of sucking slides unwittingly over into something else. "At origin aggressiveness is almost synonymous with activity," says D.W. Winnicott, but the advent of teeth and the reaction they produce hasten the development of concern.[106] To be bitten is alarming and

---

[105] Lewis Carroll, *Alice in Wonderland,* p. 12.
[106] "Aggression in Relation to Emotional Development," in Winnicott, *Through Paediatrics to Psycho-Analysis,* p. 204.

painful, and we react to it with wariness. "Once bitten, twice shy."

The erotic aspect of the mouth, which Freud took as an indication that the pleasure of the oral stage was primarily sexual, extends to the teeth.

Le menu que je préfère	[The menu I prefer
C'est la chair de votre cou	is the flesh of your neck]

sings Georges Brassens in *"J'ai rendezvous avec vous."* The love bite says, as adults sometimes say to small children, and babies no doubt feel about their mothers, "You're good enough to eat"; the act of eating becomes an embrace. The loving bite reaches its ultimate expression in the image of the vampire, where sexual desire and hunger mingle in a blood-letting orgy, and the toothsome victim swoons in an ambivalent mix of pain and pleasure.

Chewing and Deliberation

Nibbling and gnawing, as exemplified by rat and mouse, are more persistent and less dramatic forms of jaw- and toothwork than tearing and taking a bite, working away at something in a remorseless erosion (from Latin *rodere,* whence also rodent).

A bad feeling gnaws away at us. With the molars biting becomes chewing and involves time and patience. In our hasty and restless way of life much indigestion is caused by neglect of mastication. Vegetable matter especially requires thorough grinding and mixing with saliva to become a suitable substance for the gastric juices to work on. At the end of the nineteenth century, in his late forties, Horace Fletcher of the United States of America discovered chewing and acquired greatly improved health, maximizing the efficiency of his metabolism and reducing his food intake. This was Fletcherism.[107]

The rhythmic working of jaws and molars cannot be performed against a background of feelings of urgency; it requires a deliberate, repetitive perseverance. The slow penetration of the food by enzy-

---

[107] See Barbara Griggs, *The Food Factor: An Account of the Nutrition Revolution,* pp. 24f.

matic fluid means going over and over a thing, breaking it down, grinding it up, ruminating reflectively, rhythmically, unhurried, like a cow in a meadow. Impatience disrupts this placid process, driving us to jump to conclusions, swallow things whole.

A woman who was always breathlessly bounding from one topic to another in analytic sessions, and who regularly began her account of her week's events while still taking off her coat, dreamed that after evacuating her bowels she saw that her feces in the lavatory bowl contained chunks of carrot. What was taken in was expelled without being fully digested. This would have required chewing things over more and allowing time for her juices to get to work on them, but her feelings of panic created a pressure to fill the space quickly and "bolt her food."

The process of analysis is in large part one of assimilating unconscious contents, something that necessarily happens slowly. To chew thoroughly is also to savor, to get the maximum of flavor as well as food value. At this stage the food lingers in at least partial consciousness before disappearing down the throat into the hidden realm below.

Swallowing it

Swallowing is reversible only by emergency action, though Roman banqueters learned, as modern bulimics have, to exploit the safety valve of vomiting. The neck connects the head, in which we commonly locate consciousness, with the trunk, the mouth with the stomach. The inside of the mouth is highly sensitive to taste and texture. Unless we are very absent-minded we know what we put into it, and our taste buds then verify that we are eating what we expected. Once it is swallowed it is out of sight and largely out of mind; we are usually only aware of its presence if it causes us physical or psychological discomfort.

The *pretas* or hungry ghosts, who occupy one of the six realms depicted in the Tibetan wheel of life, are characterized by exceedingly thin necks. Presumably they can taste and chew, but they are deficient in swallowing and can't get much into their bodies, can't assimilate, so they remain empty and wanting, always grasping. The opposite kind of problem is reflected in the expression, "He swallowed it!"—where swallowing is apparently all too easy, and chewing-over deficient. When we swallow an unlikely story we have cheated ourselves. It will have an effect on us, but it is unlikely to nourish. Throat problems can mean that we have gulped down unpleasant experiences and emotions, swallowed our anger or tears, pushed them out of consciousness into the dark place below, or that they've stuck in our gullet.

The Mysterious Gut

Once food has been swallowed it enters the long passage of the gut where it is subject to the unconscious mechanical process of peristalsis, and to various secretions, helped by the functions of the pancreas, liver and gall bladder.

The dark interior of the gut is a place of mystery to most people, and there is much popular confusion regarding the location of the lower digestive organs. The word "stomach" comes from the Greek *stoma,* meaning mouth, and in ancient times *stomachos* signified the throat. A certain vagueness is characteristic of the use of "stomach," along with its nursery form, "tummy," and few people can correctly point to it, often indicating the lower abdomen which houses the intestines. An elderly man of my acquaintance insisted he had a pain in his stomach when he was actually suffering from hemorrhoids. This may have been a euphemism on his part, but still illustrates the imprecision of the term in popular usage.

Precisely the obscurity of what goes on in the "belly" (Old English *belig,* bag, purse, bellows) or even *where* it is, makes it a fitting image of the unconscious. The belly of the fish or whale is the underworld, where the sun goes at night; it is where heroes find themselves on the night sea journey. When Jonah was swallowed by the whale he cried out to God "from the belly of hell."

> I am cast out of thy sight . . . .
> The waters compassed me about, even to the soul: the depth closed me round about, the weeds were wrapped about my head.

I went down to the bottoms of the mountains; the earth with her
bars was about me for ever. (Jon. 2:4-6)

The word "belly," like corresponding terms in various languages,
covers intestines but also the uterus. The Greek *gaster,* from which
we have "gastric" and "gastritis," signified stomach, belly or womb.
Freud pointed out how young children wrestling with the perplex-
ing question of where babies come from, having sometimes been
told that they or some younger sibling came from "mummy's
tummy," confound the reproductive with the digestive functions,
assuming that something is ingested through the mouth, transformed and then passed out through the anus as an infant.

The hidden nature of the operations of the gut provides great
scope for the imagination. The teasing suggestion that swallowing a
cherry stone will lead to a cherry tree growing inside can be a
source of anxiety and wonderment, and what must one eat in order
to grow a baby? A widespread mythologem informs us of the
archetypal nature of these fantasies that eating leads to birth. The
Egyptian sky goddess Nut, for example, regularly devours her
children, the heavenly bodies, which emerge again from her belly.
The Great Mother, womb and tomb, embodies the endless process
of existence whereby things come into being eventually to disappear, creating at one end and destroying at the other.

Digestion in the gut involves churning (in the stomach) and
propulsion, but also chemical procedures that require heat, the biological prototype of cooking. In Chinese medicine hot food is generally preferred, to assist the process of inner combustion. Cold
food has to be heated by the body before the enzymatic breakdown
can take place, and this of course uses more energy. We say of fire
that it consumes. According to Herodotus, "The Egyptians believe
fire to be a living creature which devours whatever it gets and,
when it has eaten enough, dies with the food it feeds on."[108] The
fire of the digestive system, like the alchemist's furnace, must be
kept going throughout the process.

---

[108] *The Histories,* 3.16, p. 210.

Close to the stomach is the solar plexus, a radiating network of nerves; at the level of the subtle body the chakra located in this region governs our emotional life. Thus the stomach is particularly sensitive to complaints arising from undigested emotions. We may experience them as butterflies, sickness, a feeling of being hit in this delicate region, or a short burst of indigestion. Habitual problems of this kind can evolve into chronic gastritis or ulcers.

The stomach stores the food, further breaks it down with the enzymes pepsin and rennin, and churns it to a pulp known as chyme, related to the Greek *chymos,* meaning juice or sap, and *cheein,* to pour. The solid matter is dissolved for subsequent coagulation, converges for later separation. The stomach is a place of holding, of turning things over, but without the conscious control we exercise over the jaw muscles. If what has been taken in is poisonous or otherwise unacceptable, can't after all be stomached, it will be forcefully ejected, *re*jected, thrown back the way it came. Vomiting can mean rejecting, but also regurgitating, bringing back for re-use without properly digesting.

Most of the absorption of the blended, semiliquid chyme takes place in the small and large intestines, where it passes through the walls of the twenty-eight to thirty feet of tube. Here is the innermost mystery, the quiet climax of the assimilative process, where the boundary between the introjected contents of the alimentary canal and the rest of the receiving body is permeable. Without our knowing it, crucial metabolic transformations are now taking place. As the undulating muscular movement carries the material on, what can be is absorbed, and what can't continues on to be eliminated, along with other waste products such as dead bacteria and excretions which have performed their task. In astrology, the intestines are ruled by Virgo, the sign of detailed discrimination, but this is a discrimination that happens unconsciously.

Shit and Shadow

What is left at the end of the digestive process is an indiscriminate mess of rejected matter.

> The second law of thermodynamics clearly states that the low entropy and intricate, dynamic organization of a living system can only function through the excretion of low-grade products and low-grade energy to the environment.[109]

Returned to the environment, our waste again becomes part of the cyclic process, feeding the ground for future plant growth.

As well as being seen as expulsion of waste, defecation can also be considered a form of expression. Constipation may mean keeping too much in, while "verbal diarrhea" is overexpression. A writer who was having difficulty getting on with a book, going through a characteristic creative depression, kept dreaming of sitting and straining on the lavatory. The night before the words came bursting out she had to hurry to the dream toilet for fear of being caught short—another example of giving birth through the anus.

Feces are in a sense deeply personal, an expression of the individual. In many species, in accordance with nature's economic use of materials, feces serve as a territorial marker, communicating distinctly that *I* was here and no other. This end-product or rather byproduct emerges again into visibility from the inner darkness. Its form, color, texture and smell can be noted. Its expulsion, in adults, is normally under conscious muscular control—but we can choose not to look at it, and have devised disposal systems that rapidly take it out of sight. Children of a certain age allude to it in the certainty of annoying adults by breaking a taboo.

To the still smaller child it is a source of wonderment and entertainment, and a focus of will power, frustration and rage, as the child learns sphincter control at the insistence of grown-ups. To become a healthy as well as a properly functioning, socially acceptable person it must know what to reject. This substance which is so very personal is also nevertheless other, belongs on the outside, and must be kept at a distance for reasons of hygiene and propriety. It becomes a byword for all that is obnoxious, hated ("What a shit he is!"); it is despised, meaningless ("Utter crap!") or bad news

---

[109] J. Lovelock, *Gaia: A New Look at Life on Earth,* p. 27.

("Shit!"). We wish to sever our connection with it; it is what could not be integrated into our sense of who we are, though we have to deal with it on a daily basis, our personal shame and shadow.

The bathroom scenes of our dreams, sometimes a particularly persistent theme for those who consciously lead very "clean" lives, are often accompanied by severe embarrassment, doors that won't shut, feelings of exposure. The flush won't work, there is shit everywhere. "It seems I have to clean it up myself. I can't seem to find any tools"—an Augean task. We feel filthy, contaminated. Yet Paracelsus once brandished this very filth to demonstrate the *prima materia,* the starting point of the alchemical opus; in it there is often to be glimpsed some priceless jewel, a ring or gold coins, a glimmer of light in the dark *massa confusa.* In what has been rejected lies the potential for enlightenment. It provides fertilizer for the garden of the soul, and in this sense is also food. The end of the inner alchemical process of moistening, heating, dissolving, separating and congealing is also a place of beginning, and typically where we start the work of analysis.

In his essay "Character and Anal Eroticism," Freud discusses the widespread juxtaposition of money and excrement in myths, fairy tales and dreams.[110] He interprets this connection reductively, as a projection onto money of what was formerly associated with anal pleasures, feces being our first "gift" to the world. He remarks in passing on the striking contrast between the most esteemed and the most despised, but without valuing it as paradox or metaphor. As such it has a bearing on his own work, which found reward in investigating the murky darkness of the personal shadow.

Nourishment and Value

Apart from simply maintaining the body and its functions, physical food provides us with the energy we need to live our lives. Where does the energy from dream food go? It depends on who is doing the eating.

---

[110] *Standard Edition,* vol. 9, pp. 169ff.

A dreamer arrives at a hotel and finds her way to a room that feels familiar. She takes it to be *her* room. Breakfast is laid out on a table, apparently for her, but the bed is occupied by a couple who insist it is *their* room (and therefore their breakfast), and tell her to leave. She goes off to find the office, where a fat, unhealthy-looking youth is demanding a special diet. At the end of the dream the dreamer apparently remains hungry, but the couple, associated with the parental complexes, presumably ate the breakfast, and the demanding and picky teenage animus is already overfed. The breakfast is not transformed into energy disposable by the dreamer's ego, but the "parents" have more energy for rejection, and the youth, if he gets his way, will have all the more unhealthy energy for making demands. The libido is flowing into these autonomous figures so they can be primed for further activity.

Another woman dreamed she was queuing for dinner at a professional conference. A big fat man, an old friend in the dream but unknown to the waking ego, came to greet her. She went to hug him and lost her place in the queue, but he, having already eaten, laughed and said she could eat when the long queue had died down. This however would not be possible, as she had shortly to address the conference. Again, the feminine ego is starved while the obese man, associated here with the professional standing and intellectual function of the dreamer, misunderstands her circumstances. An overfed animus also appeared in the dream of a third woman, whose sleep was often spoiled by uncontrollable busy thoughts. In this case the unknown fat man had set an alarm clock to wake her in the early hours. She needed to wake up to his weight problem.

Some dreams tell us what needs feeding. Neglected psychic factors often personify themselves as underfed figures, starving animals, screaming babies. At the dream level feeding *is* giving attention, that is, directing psychic energy toward what needs it. The dreamer may fail to find food, as William Burroughs discovers repeatedly in the "Land of the Dead,"[111] a location in his dreams

---

[111] *My Education: A Book of Dreams,* p. 11.

where "there is always difficulty in obtaining breakfast or any food for that matter." When the dreamer does manage to eat it is an indication that something is nearing consciousness. This is why Edward Edinger remarks, "Whenever food is offered one in a dream, the general rule is that it should be eaten no matter how unpleasant it seems."[112]

While we do "take things in" from the external world, analysis is largely about the process of assimilating unconscious contents, that is, things that we already know somewhere, but don't know we know, including hidden assumptions about things "out there." This is the process whereby the psyche "eats itself."

Sometimes there is a great sense of release when some complex that has been secretly damming up energy at last becomes part of our conscious picture of ourselves. Much of the time the process is more gradual, a progressive filling out of our self-image, incorporating all kinds of elements that we had hitherto projected onto other people. The projection of positive elements can lead to low self-esteem and envy; when negative components are projected we become involved in futile and destructive battles. When we reclaim these projected contents we acquire more body, more psychological substance; we fill out our own space more fully, with greater respect for our own complexity. We also see others more clearly, often with less blame, and can find better ways of relating to them.

It would be wrong, though, to give the impression that we arrive at a point where there is no more such work to be done; there is a danger of after-dinner smugness setting in, a know-it-all feeling. If we are not to set ourselves up for a fall, we must continually respect the vastness of the unconscious psyche, recognition that things slip out of consciousness too, that the tail-eating process of eating and being eaten goes on all the time.

---

[112] *Anatomy of the Psyche,* p. 111.

5
Fat, Body Image and Self-Image

The thinness and fatness of dream figures can depict the uneven distribution of psychic energy, personifying on the one hand the starved, on the other the overfed elements of our being. When the dreamer is represented as obese it may indicate that the ego has arrogated to itself more than its share of psychic resources and become inflated. It is, however, the issue of fat in waking life that currently causes us great concern.

In times when famine threatens, probably the norm throughout the history of human experience, fatness is an achievement implying success in obtaining the means of survival and an insurance against hard times, and therefore tends to be highly valued. A recent review of relevant studies found a direct relationship between high socioeconomic status and obesity in developing, that is poorer societies, and the authors suggest that "it may be a sign of health and wealth in [these] societies, the opposite of its meaning in developed countries."[113]

A study of captive female macaque monkeys determined that, regardless of age and pregnancy, the highest-ranking females were the fattest.[114] Writing in the early 1970s, Hilde Bruch remarked on "the paradox that in affluent societies obesity is commonly associated with poverty and lower-class status."

> [Women] who had been poor immigrants who had suffered hunger during their early lives . . . did not understand why anyone should object to a child's being big and fat, which to them indicated success and freedom from want.[115]

---

[113] Jeffery Sobal and Albert J. Stunkard, "Socioeconomic Status and Obesity: A Review of the Literature."

[114] See Meredith F. Small, "Body Fat, Rank and Nutritional Status in a Captive Group of Rhesus Macaques."

[115] *Eating Disorders,* pp. 14f.

Fat has often meant wealth, to be "fat and flourishing" (Ps. 92:14), to "eat the fat of the land" (Gen. 45:18), and we speak of being "fair, fat and forty." To have a "fair round belly with good capon lin'd"[116] was in Shakespeare's day to have reached the age corresponding to the planet Jupiter, acclaimed by astrologers as the Great Benefic, and to be entitled to spread oneself out a bit, having become a stout citizen and acquired some solidity and substance. In contrast, the modern Greek word for thin, *adynatos,* conveys the deep-rooted fears attaching to a lack of physical bulk, for its original meaning is "weak."

For people in rich societies, where weight can be acquired easily, slimness rather than corpulence is considered an achievement, and even women from poor backgrounds, after decades of televised images of desirable slimness, tend to value being thin. Granted that there are some cases of obesity which cannot be modified by a change in eating habits, much overweight is simply a question of succumbing, for one reason or another, to the easy availability of food. Under such conditions nature no longer ensures that we do not overeat, and we have to take responsibility for this ourselves.

We have seen how compelling are the images of the bountiful mother, who feeds us with the best victuals without any effort on our part: the fruit that offers itself for us to pick, the cornucopia, the self-spreading table, the Land of Cockayne with its ready-made confections and self-cooking pigs. We have done our best to create Cockayne in the supermarket with its ready-cooked meals and self-basting turkeys, open from early morning to late at night, where for those who can pay the main problem is one of choice.

Apart from simply pleasing the palate, the sheer availability of food means that it becomes a ready stand-in for other forms of satisfaction, a substitute for paying attention to emotional needs and conflicts. For the compulsive eater it is as if, when there are feelings of anger or sadness, or longings that are not easily satisfied, the "too-good" mother offers her painless answer: "Never mind,

---

116 *As You Like It,* act 2, scene 7.

have another piece of cake." We have learned to expect and demand instant gratification, instant credit, instant solutions to problems, but to the extent that this is possible it puts us at risk of regression.

In the distant past the urgent need for our ancestors to feed themselves stimulated the development of human skills and consciousness. The reverse is also true; that is, when there is nothing to contend with we readily become lazy and infantilized. The return to paradise, however, is barred to us. We may dally awhile in gardens of indulgence, but in doing so we run into new problems of dependency, in addition to, in the case of food, those attendant upon overweight. The biscuit tin is so easy to reach into. It is more difficult but more satisfying in the long run to turn to the inner cornucopia, the food of the psyche, the stuff whose digestion leads to consciousness.

Thinness is seen as desirable when it is easy to get fat. Perhaps the obsessive pursuit of slimness in our society is in part an expression of our revulsion at the grossness and psychic inflation of our materialistic age. The extreme abstention demonstrated by sufferers of anorexia nervosa recreates or parodies the world-denying asceticism which in the past has been practiced for the purpose of spiritual development. Plato located in the stomach region that part of the soul which related to the appetitive or desirous nature, seeing it as an unfortunate necessity, a beast to be fed in order that the nobler aspects of human nature could function.[117] Sometimes a secret longing for a more spiritualized life lurks in the flight from body weight and the instinctual demands of the gut. The pattern of out-of-control swinging between the opposites of abstinence and excess also echoes in a distorted way the old religious calendar with its fast days and feast days.

It is primarily women who are tormented by the desire to be slim, leading to compulsive dieting, alternation between stuffing and starving, and in extreme cases to anorexia and bulimia. Eating disorders among men are on the increase, but having no experience

---

[117] *Timaeus*, 70 Df.

in this area I must limit myself here to the problems of women. There are many layers to women's concern with their body image which can be a major factor in a problematical relationship to food. Among them are the ancient interaction between men's sexual response to visual cues and the high value women place on relationships; the contemporary emphasis on superficial appearance as opposed to substance; women's search for a new inner image; and the tendency of body image to stand in for self-image where the latter is negative or inadequate.

Many women driven to pursue the elusive ideal figure are in the grip of an archcritic who projects into their body tissue their inability to match up to impossible or inappropriate standards, incompatible with the realities of the flesh, so that instead of tackling their insecurities they fight their bodies. This critic steps in with his negative judgments where a woman's sense of herself as a feminine being is in some way lacking, and it is he who starves the anorexic. The current epidemic of dieting and eating disorders constitutes a widespread insecurity among women, which can be seen as a shift in the collective toward new developments in feminine consciousness. At the individual level it is driven by a sense of dissatisfaction which, when rightly related to, acts as an impetus to self-discovery.

Since meals have always been an important ritual in family life and a focus for the socialization of the young, they also provide an opportunity for resistance to the parental culture as part of the child's process of seeking self-definition. Even where much of the ritual has broken down and eating patterns are less regular, eating can still be loaded with parents' concerns and anxiety, so that from the perspective of the child food may be experienced as an instrument of maternal control, an invasion of personal space which the child has not yet managed to claim.

Where traditional expectations of woman's role are no longer respected, and the all-competent, sexually desirable superwoman image is far from most women's reality, there is no easy passage into womanhood. Amid pressures to meet family expectations, to succeed in study and in job stakes, to keep up with peer groups and to attract potential partners, the key to discovering her true individuality and vocation is particularly hard for a young woman to find. Often then her self-image is composed largely of negatives, of not being quite what she believes others want of her, and since the body symbolizes our conscious identity it provides a tangible object of self-improvement on which the relentless inner critic can focus.

Many women still see the acquisition of, and merging with, a partner as a solution to all their problems. This may block the development of full individuality, which is the only way truly satisfying relationships can develop. The tremendous current emphasis on sexuality as a key component in the success of an intimate relationship can create further pressure and confusion. A few centuries ago in various cultures, the young woman who did not feel drawn to marriage, or in whom the spiritual dimension took precedence, had a socially acceptable alternative in celibate religious orders. Nowadays the nonmenstruating anorexic, who typically avoids sex as well as food, and the obese woman with her protective layer of fat, may be seeking that alternative in the body.

It seems to me that new developments in feminine consciousness have been struggling to emerge for a long time, and that eating problems have replaced hysteria as a medicalized expression of woman's malaise and need for change. While this is a collective problem, insight and consciousness develop primarily through the attempts of individual women to bring these psychic forces to awareness.

Eating problems, like many other distressing symptoms, manifest the psyche's need to be seen, honored and loved. The more the body is manipulated and abused through deprivation, binging and purging, the deeper the feelings of floundering and loss of control. When the attention shifts from physical weight to inner reality, however bleak, unworthy or frightening this may feel at the outset, the unseen body of the psyche begins to be nourished, and the possibility of a new, more friendly relationship with the physical body can emerge. Weight is then no longer such a problem.

Each person is born unique and has particular contributions to make. The inner seed of individuality knows darkly what kind of fruit is its destiny to produce and what kind of environment it will flourish in. But this knowledge is often deeply hidden, and attempts to mold ourselves into some ideal taken from collective consciousness, projected onto the body, set us against ourselves. Out of this struggle with what we are not, the real person can emerge into the light.

Bibliography

Aeschylus, *Prometheus Bound.* In *Greek Tragedies,* vol. 1. Trans. David Grene. Ed. David Grene, Richmond Lattimore. Chicago: University of Chicago Press, 1960.

Anderson, William, and Hicks, Clive. *Green Man: The Archetype of Our Oneness with the Earth.* San Francisco: HarperCollins, 1990.

Angus, S. *The Mystery-Religions and Christianity.* London: John Murray, 1925.

Athenaeus. *Deipnosophistae (The Learned Banquet).* Trans. C.B. Gulick. Cambridge, MA: Loeb Classical Library, Harvard University Press, 1927-41.

Benveniste, Emile. *Indo-European Language and Society.* Trans. Elizabeth Palmer. London: Faber and Faber, 1973.

Boysen, Sarah T., and Berntson, G.G. "Responses to Quantity: Perceptual Versus Cognitive Mechanisms in Chimpanzees *(Pan Troglodytes)."* In *Journal of Experimental Psychology and Animal Behavior Processes,* vol. 21, no. 1 (1995).

Brillat-Savarin, Jean-Anthelme. *Physiologie du Goût.* Paris: Pierre Waleffe, 1967.

Bruch, Hilde. *Eating Disorders.* London: Routledge and Kegan Paul, 1974.

Burkert, Walter. *Greek Religion, Archaic and Classical.* Trans. John Raffan. Oxford: Basil Blackwell, 1987.

Burroughs, William. *My Education: A Book of Dreams.* New York: Penguin, 1995.

_____. *The Naked Lunch.* New York: Grove Press, 1959.

The Cambridge Encyclopaedia of Human Evolution. Ed. S. Jones, R. Martin, D. Pilbeam. Cambridge: Cambridge University Press, 1992.

Campbell, Joseph. *The Masks of God: Occidental Mythology.* New York: Viking Press, 1964.

_____. *The Masks of God: Primitive Mythology.* New York: Viking Penguin, 1959.

_____. *The Way of the Animal Powers: Historical Atlas of World Mythology,* vol. 1. London: Times Books, 1984.

Carmichael, Elizabeth, and Sayer, Chloë. *The Skeleton at the Feast: The Day of the Dead in Mexico.* London: British Museum Press, 1991.

Carroll, Lewis. *Alice in Wonderland.* London: Everyman Classics, J.M. Dent and Sons, 1961.

Chaitow, Leon. *Stone Age Diet.* London: Macdonald Optima, 1987.

Coon, Carleton S. *The History of Man from the First Human to Primitive Culture and Beyond.* London: Jonathan Cape, 1957.

Courlander, Harold. *The King's Drum and Other African Stories.* London: Rupert Hart-Davis (imprint of HarperCollins Publishers Limited), 1963.

Dally, Peter, and Gomez, Joan. *Anorexia Nervosa.* London: William Heinemann, 1979.

Detienne, Marcel, and Vernant, Jean-Pierre. *The Cuisine of Sacrifice Among the Greeks.* Trans. Paula Wissing. Chicago: University of Chicago Press, 1989.

de Vries, Ad. *Dictionary of Symbols and Imagery.* Rev. ed. Amsterdam: North Holland Publishing Company, 1976.

Edinger, Edward F. *Anatomy of the Psyche: Alchemical Symbolism in Psychotherapy.* La Salle, IL: Open Court, 1985.

_____. *The Mysterium Lectures: A Journey through C.G. Jung's* Mysterium Coniunctionis. Toronto: Inner City Books, 1995.

Eliade, Mircea. *A History of Religious Ideas.* 3 vols. Chicago: University of Chicago Press, 1978-1985.

Elias, Norbert. *The Civilizing Process: The History of Manners.* Trans. Edmund Jephcott. Oxford: Basil Blackwell, Oxford, 1982.

The Epic of Gilgamesh. Trans. N.K. Sandars. Harmondsworth, UK: Penguin, 1972.

Frazer, J.G. *The Golden Bough: A Study in Magic and Religion.* Abridged ed. London: Macmillan, 1957.

Freud, Sigmund. *The Standard Edition of the Complete Works of Sigmund Freud.* 24 vols. Trans. James Strachey. London: Hogarth Press, 1953-1974.

Funk and Wagnalls. *Standard Dictionary of Folklore, Mythology & Legend.* London: New English Library, 1975.

Garner, D.M.; Garfinkel, P.E.; Schwartz, D.; and Thompson, M. "Cultural Expectation of Thinness in Women." In *Psychological Reports,* vol. 47 (1980).

Gibson, Thomas. "Meat Sharing As a Political Ritual: Forms of Transaction Versus Modes of Subsistence." In *Hunters and Gatherers 2: Property, Power and Ideology.* Ed. Tim Ingold, David Riches, James Woodburn. Oxford: Berg, 1988.

Goodall, Jane. *The Chimpanzees of Gombe : Patterns of Behaviour.* Harvard: Belknap Press of Harvard University Press, 1986.

Graves, Robert. *The White Goddess.* London: Faber and Faber, 1961.

Graves, Robert, and Patai, Raphael. *Hebrew Myths: The Book of Genesis.* London: Cassell, 1964.

Griggs, Barbara. *The Food Factor: An Account of the Nutrition Revolution.* Harmondsworth, UK: Penguin, 1986.

Grimm Brothers. *The Complete Grimm's Fairy Tales.* London: Routledge and Kegan Paul, 1975.

Herodotus. *The Histories.* Trans. Aubrey de Sélincourt. Rev. A.R. Burn. London: Penguin, 1972.

Hesiod. *Works and Days* and *Theogony.* Trans. H.G. Evelyn-White. Cambridge, MA: Loeb Classical Library, Harvard University Press, 1914.

Hippocratic Writings. Trans. J. Chadwick and W.N. Mann. Ed. G.E.R. Lloyd. Harmondsworth, UK: Penguin, 1983.

Homer. *The Iliad.* Trans. E.V. Rieu. Harmondsworth, UK: Penguin, 1950.

———. *The Odyssey.* Trans. A.T. Murray. Cambridge, MA: Loeb Classical Library, Harvard University Press, 1919.

The I Ching or Book of Changes. Trans. from Chinese into German by Richard Wilhelm, rendered into English by Cary F. Baynes. London: Routledge and Kegan Paul, 1951.

Isaac, Glynn L.I., and Sept, Jeanne M. "Long-Term History of the Human Diet." In *The Eating Disorders.* Ed. B.J. Blinder, B.F. Chaitin, R. Goldstein. New York: PMA Publishing Corp., 1988.

James, E.O. *The Cult of the Mother Goddess.* Thames and Hudson, London, 1959.

Jung, C.G. *The Collected Works* (Bollingen Series XX). 20 vols. Trans. R.F.C. Hull. Ed. H. Read, M. Fordham, G. Adler, Wm. McGuire. Princeton: Princeton University Press, 1953-1979.

———. *Dream Analysis* (Bollingen Series XCIX). Ed. Wm. McGuire. London: Routledge and Kegan Paul, 1984.

———. *Memories, Dreams, Reflections.* Trans. Richard and Clara Winston. Ed. Aniela Jaffé. London: Fontana Library, 1971.

Jung, C.G., and Kerényi, Carl. *Introduction to a Science of Mythology.* Trans. R.F.C. Hull. London: Routledge and Kegan Paul, 1951.

Kerényi, Carl. *Prometheus: Archetypal Image of Human Existence.* Trans. Ralph Manheim. London: Thames and Hudson, 1963.

Klesges, R.C., Klein, M.L., and Klesges, L.M. "The Relationship Between Changes in Body Weight and Changes in Psychological Functioning." In *Appetite,* vol. 19 (1992).

Lacey, J.I., Kagan, J., Lacey, B.C., and Moss, H.A. "The Visceral Level: Situational Determinants and Behavioural Correlates of Autonomic Response Patterns." In *Expression of the Emotions in Man.* Ed. P.H. Knapp. New York: International University Press, 1963.

Layard, John. *A Celtic Quest: Sexuality and Soul in Individuation.* Zürich: Spring Publications, 1975.

Leakey, Richard, and Lewin, Roger. *People of the Lake: Man, His Origins, Nature and Future.* Harmondsworth, UK: Penguin, 1981.

Lee, Richard B., and DeVore, Irven , eds. *Man the Hunter.* New York: Aldine Publishing Co., 1968.

Lévi-Strauss, Claude. *The Raw and the Cooked.* Harmondsworth, UK: Penguin, 1986.

Lizot, Jacques. *Tales of the Yanomami: Daily Life in the Venezuelan Forest.* Trans. Ernest Simon. Cambridge: Cambridge University Press, 1985.

London, Jack. *The Call of the Wild* and *White Fang.* Ware, U.K.: Wordsworth Classics, 1992.

López-Pedraza, Rafael. *Hermes and His Children.* Revised ed. Einsiedeln, Switzerland: Daimon Verlag, 1989.

Lovelock, J.E. *Gaia: A New Look at Life on Earth.* Oxford: Oxford University Press, 1979.

Mackenzie, Donald A. *China and Japan* (Myths and Legends Series). London: Senate (Studio Editions), 1994.

McLuhan, T.C., ed. *Touch the Earth: A Self-Portrait of Indian Existence.* London: Abacus (Sphere Books), 1973.

Mars, Gerald, and Mars, Valerie. "Two Contrasting Dining Styles." In *Food, Culture and History,* vol. 1 (1993).

Marvel, Andrew. *Selected Poems.* Ed. Bill Hutchings. Manchester: Fyfield Books, 1979.

Montanari, Massimo. *The Culture of Food.* Trans. Carl Ipsen. Oxford: Basil Blackwell, 1994.

Morgan, Elaine. *The Aquatic Ape.* London: Souvenir Press, 1982.

_____. *The Descent of Woman.* London: Souvenir Press, 1972.

_____. *The Scars of Evolution: What Our Bodies Tell Us About Human Origins.* London: Souvenir Press, 1990.

Neumann, Erich. *The Great Mother: An Analysis of the Archetype* (Bollingen Series XLVII). Princeton: Princeton University Press, 1972.

_____. *The Origins and History of Consciousness* (Bollingen Series XLII). Princeton: Princeton University Press, 1970.

Onians, R.B. *The Origins of European Thought.* Cambridge: Cambridge University Press, 1951.

Orbach, Susie. *Fat is a Feminist Issue.* New York: Paddington Press, 1978.

Otto, Walter F. *Dionysos: Myth and Cult.* Dallas, TX: Spring Publications, 1981.

Ovid. *Metamorphoses.* Trans. Frank Justus Miller. 2 vols. Cambridge, MA: Loeb Classical Library, Harvard University Press, 1916.

_____. *The Doctrines of Pythagoras.* Trans. A.D. Melville. Oxford: Oxford University Press, 1986.

The Oxford Companion to Animal Behaviour. Ed. D. McFarland. Oxford: Oxford University Press, 1987.

Page, D., trans. *Sappho and Alcaeus: An Introduction to the Study of Ancient Lesbian Poetry.* Oxford: Clarendon Press, 1955.

Partridge, Eric. *Origins: A Short Etymological Dictionary of Modern English.* Routledge and Kegan Paul, London, 1966. (First pubd. 1958.)

Pindar. *The Odes of Pindar.* Trans. Maurice Bowra. Harmondsworth, UK: Penguin, 1969.

Plato. *The Republic of Plato.* Trans. Francis Macdonald Cornford. Oxford: Oxford University Press, 1941.

_____. *Timaeus.* Trans. R. G. Bury. Cambridge, MA: Loeb Classical Library, Harvard University Press, 1929.

Popol Vuh: The Sacred Book of the Ancient Quiché Maya. English version by Delia Goetz and Sylvanus G. Morley, from the Spanish translation by Adrián Recinos. London: William Hodge, 1951.

Porphyry. *On Abstinence from Animal Food.* Trans. Thomas Taylor. Ed. and intro. Esmé Wynne-Taylor. London: Centaur Press, 1965.

The Qur'an. Trans. M.H. Shakir. New York: Tahrike Tarsile Qur'an, 1988.

Schwartz, Charles. *Money Symbolism: The Psychological Standards of Value That Back Money.* Diploma Thesis, C.G. Jung Institute, Zürich, 1978.

Skeat, Walter W. *The Concise Dictionary of English Etymology.* Ware, UK: Wordsworth Editions, 1993.

Slochower, Joyce; Kaplan, Sharon P.; and Mann, Lisa. "The Effects of Life Stress and Weight on Mood and Eating." in *Appetite,* vol. 2 (1981).

Small, Meredith F. "Body Fat, Rank, and Nutritional Status in a Captive Group of Rhesus Macaques." In *International Journal of Primatology,* vol. 2 (1981).

Sobal, Jeffery, and Stunkard, Albert J. "Socioeconomic Status and Obesity: A Review of the Literature." In *Psychological Bulletin,* vol. 105, no. 2 (1989).

Spence, Lewis. *The Religion of Ancient Mexico.* London: Watts, 1945.

Spencer, Colin. *The Heretic's Feast: A History of Vegetarianism.* London: Fourth Estate, 1993.

Tournier, Michel. *Le Médianoche Amoureux.* Paris: Gallimard, 1989.

Turnbull, Colin M. *The Forest People.* London: Chatto and Windus, 1961.

The Upanishads. Trans. Juan Mascaró. Harmondsworth, UK: Penguin, 1965.

Visser, Margaret. *Much Depends on Dinner.* London: Penguin, 1989.

_____. *The Rituals of Dinner.* London: Penguin, 1992.

von Franz, Marie-Louise. *The Feminine in Fairy Tales.* Dallas, TX: Spring Publications, 1972.

Whitman, John. *The Psychic Power of Plants.* London: W.H. Allen (Star Books), 1975.

Williams, C.A.S. *Outlines of Chinese Symbolism and Art Motives.* 3rd ed. New York: Dover, 1976.

Wilson, Hilary. *Egyptian Food and Drink.* Aylesbury, UK: Shire Publications, 1988.

Winnicott, D.W. *Through Paediatrics to Psycho-Analysis.* London: Hogarth and The Institute of Psycho-Analysis, 1982.

Woodburn, James. "Egalitarian Societies." In *Man* (N.S.) vol. 17 (1982).

Woodman, Marion. *Addiction to Perfection: The Still Unravished Bride.* Toronto: Inner City Books, 1982.

Yannissopoulou, Maria. *L'Expression des Relations Sociales dans le Partage de la Nourriture au Village de Potamia.* Dissertation for Maitrise d'Ethnologie, Université Paris VII, U.E.R. d'Ethnologie, 1981.

Index

Freud/Freudian, 19, 103
"Character and Anal Eroticism," 109
fruit, 16-18, 34-47. *See also by name*

Gaia, 11, 13, 37-38
gathering, 32-33, 37, 46-47, 65, 73
Genesis, Book of, 35, 45-46, 68, 113
giants, 28-29
Gibson, Thomas: "Meat Sharing," 56
Gilgamesh Epic, 69
gods/goddesses, 25-28, 60-61, 72-75, 86, 88
as complexes, 27-28
sacrifices to, 17, 25-30, 36, 57, 60-67, 79
Golden Age, 35-36, 44
grain, 65-76. *See also* corn; rice; wheat
Mother, 72, 75
Graves, Robert: *The White Goddess,* 43
Great Mother (Grain/Corn/Earth, etc.), 11-14, 25, 27, 43, 72-75, 102, 106
Greece/Greeks, 17, 35-36, 38, 41, 48-49, 57-61, 64-65, 72, 76, 79, 83, 86-87, 92-93
Green Man, 97
Griggs, Barbara: *The Food Factor,* 103
guilt, 18, 36, 63-64, 78, 80
Gwynne, Nell, 42

Hades, 39, 74-76
Hainuwele, 67
Hallowell, A.I.: "Bear Ceremonialism," 63
Hansel and Gretel, 14-15, 43
Hardy, Alister, 31
Harris, D.R.: "Human Diet and Subsistence," 32
Hathor, 44
head, 56-57
health food, 9. *See also* vegetarianism
Hera, 16, 37-38, 43, 86
Heracles, 43, 52, 58
Hermes, 20, 58
hero/heroism, 23-26, 28, 35, 45-55, 99, 105
Herodotus: *The Histories,* 106
Hesiod: *Theogony,* 11
Works and Days, 35, 61
Hesperides, 37, 43
Hindus, 83

Hippomenes, 41
Hole, Frank: "Reconstructing Prehistoric Diet," 32
Homer: *The Iliad,* 48-49, 58, 69
honey, 35, 98
Horus, 25, 52
hunger, 8, 13, 43, 48, 103, 112
hunting, 32-34, 37, 46-65, 80
Huxley, T.H., 31
hyena, 59

I Ching, 31, 80
Idun, 43
Incas, 57
Indians, American, 27, 57, 93
individuation, 44
instinct/instinctual, 13, 19, 66, 80
Iron Hans, 50-54
Isaiah, Book of, 35-36
Isis, 16, 52, 72
Islam, 36
Ives, Burl: "The Big Rock Candy Mountain," 43

jackal, 59
Jesus. *See* Christ
Jews/Jewish, 23, 38, 64, 78, 82, 86, 98
John, St., Apocryphal Acts, 13
Jonah, 25, 105-106
Judas, 83
Jung, C.G., 9, 27-28, 44, 54, 56, 96
Dream Analysis, 9, 27, 101
"The Meaning of Psychology for Modern Man," 61
Memories, Dreams, Reflections, 95
"The Philosophical Tree," 44
"Psychological Factors in Human Behaviour," 13
"The Psychology of the Child Archetype," 7
"A Review of the Complex Theory," 28
"Synchronicity: An Acausal Connecting Principle," 96
"Transformation Symbolism in the Mass," 30, 69

OTHER INNER CITY TITLES *(Write or phone for complete Catalogue)*

Living Jung: The Good and the Better
Daryl Sharp (Toronto) ISBN 0-919123-73-2. 128 pp. $15

The Middle Passage: From Misery to Meaning in Midlife
James Hollis (Philadelphia) ISBN 0-919123-60-0. 128 pp. $15

Eros and Pathos: Shades of Love and Suffering
Aldo Carotenuto (Rome) ISBN 0-919123-39-2. 144 pp. $16

Descent to the Goddess: A Way of Initiation for Women
Sylvia Brinton Perera (New York) ISBN 0-919123-05-8. 112 pp. $15

Addiction to Perfection: The Still Unravished Bride
Marion Woodman (Toronto) ISBN 0-919123-11-2. Illustrated. 208 pp. $18

Coming To Age: The Croning Years and Late-Life Transformation
Jane R. Prétat (Providence, RI) ISBN 0-919123-63-5. 144 pp. $16

Jungian Dream Interpretation: A Handbook of Theory and Practice
James A. Hall, M.D. (Dallas) ISBN 0-919123-12-0. 128 pp. $15

Jung Lexicon: A Primer of Terms & Concepts
Daryl Sharp (Toronto) ISBN 0-919123-48-1. Diagrams. 160 pp. $16

The Sacred Prostitute: Eternal Aspect of the Feminine
Nancy Qualls-Corbett (Birmingham) ISBN 0-919123-31-7. Illustrated. 176 pp. $18

The Mysterium Lectures: A Journey through Jung's Mysterium Coniunctionis
Edward F. Edinger (Los Angeles) ISBN 0-919123-60-0 90 illustrations 352 pp. $20

Swamplands of the Soul: New Life in Dismal Places
James Hollis (Philadelphia) ISBN 0-919123-74-0. 160 pp. $16

Prices and payment in $US (except in Canada,$Cdn)
Discounts: any 3-5 books, 10%; 6 books or more, 20%
Add Postage/Handling: 1-2 books, $2; 3-4 books, $4; 5-9 books, $8

INNER CITY BOOKS
Box 1271, Station Q, Toronto, ON M4T 2P4, Canada   (416) 927-0355